IS IT GOD
OR
COINCIDENCE?

*COMING TO GRIPS
WITH THE
UNEXPECTED WONDERS
IN LIFE*

Rob Ekno

Copy Editor – Megan Rhode
Cover Design, Mentor – David Theberge
"Spencer's Graphic" – Spencer Hersom
Back Cover Author Photo – Charmaine Cruz, *Into Life Photography*
Angel on Ice and *Five Finger Lighthouse* Photos – Rob Ekno
Photo Strip Credits – Rob Ekno, Otis N., Phil L., Matt Brown, Andy Brown, and Mike Todd

Special Thanks to: Sue, Katie, and Mary

Some names and identifying details of people described in this book have been altered to protect their privacy.

Rob Ekno
Visit my website at www.RobEkno.com

Printed in the United States of America

First Printing: August 2020
KDP

ISBN-13 978-1-7355520-0-2

CONTENTS

DEDICATION

To God

Thank You for blessing me with an amazing family and wonderful friends. I am also truly grateful for so many incredible life experiences with which You have provided me. Some of those, You have asked me to share in this book.

Whether it was enjoying my greatest victories or going through my toughest challenges, You have always been there for me. Thank You for loving me and not leaving me alone, even when I wanted absolutely nothing to do with You. You are a true friend!

It has been during my most recent trying times that our relationship has elevated to new levels. Joyfully, it continues to grow stronger daily as I focus on Your will for me.

Learning to fully trust in You has been the greatest gift that I have ever received. Hence, I can live my life in peace, knowing that I will always have everything that I need because I have You.

You're all I need!

FOREWORD

I first met Rob when he signed on as a student disc jockey at our high school radio station about 45 years ago. His creativity and willingness to work hard made him a valuable member of that crew and, as you will see in this book, those qualities have stayed with him over the decades.

The radio station was not included in the school budget, but Rob made up his mind that we were going to put it on the air anyway. We created a mobile disc jockey service that provided music for events at schools and youth groups in the area. Rob scoured the local roads for donations to bring in enough money for equipment and licensing to put the station on the air.

It is no exaggeration to say that without the 17-year-old Rob, the student radio station that is still on the air today would not ever have opened its doors. Rob always gave one hundred percent then and, as you will see in the pages of this book, he never lost that energy and willingness to give.

This book is about Rob's very personal story of his search to understand his relationship to God. Are the events of our lives coincidence or evidence of the hand of God upon us? Rob has some stories to share in this book that will, at the very least, give you something to think about in your own life.

I told Rob that I had to run my calculator twice to check on the 45 years that we have been friends. As it always is with old friends, every time we talk it is easy to pick up where we left off. But a conversation with Rob always brings something new—a new thought, a new lesson, a new way of looking at things.

I hope that when you read this book, you will get to know my friend Rob Ekno and, more importantly, that Rob's story will help you get closer to knowing God as well.

If you are searching, you will ultimately have to find your own answer. In the pages of this book, however, you will find inspiration, encouragement, and hope for the journey.

Ken Grady
Executive Producer & Co-Host
Gospel Music Today

INTRODUCTION

S hortly after I began writing this book, I started sharing its title with a number of family members, friends, and strangers alike. I don't know whether or not they were believers, but each of them could recount miraculous happenings in *their* lives that touched them, some so intensely that their eyes filled with tears. Each one—*at the time of the events* they described—had the feeling that *a power greater than themselves* had been watching over them. I could be wrong, but it seems to me that everyone has similar experiences, yet some attribute them to God and others to coincidence.

There have been numerous inspirational events and coincidental signs that I've witnessed throughout my life. However, within the past eight years, I have experienced some absolutely astounding and overwhelming coincidences. Some people call them "God shots." For me, there was one major God shot that happened in the most unexplainable way—though, at the time, I didn't realize its significance. It was the last piece of evidence that I needed, the one that made it perfectly clear that God wanted me to write this book. This is how it happened.

During three months of a recent summer, I worked as a cruise ship host in Washington, Oregon, and Alaska. After the season ended, I returned to Los Angeles and met my best friend, Johnny, for lunch at a popular local restaurant. Sitting at our table, he asked me what I was going to do now that the cruise season had ended. I told him that I wasn't sure. God had not yet given me my next assignment.

Immediately upon leaving the restaurant, I was taken aback. There was an SUV parked right in front of us. Its license plate was GODSPLN.

Shocked by both what I was seeing and its timing, I excitedly pointed out my discovery to Johnny. At nearly the same time, I grabbed my cellphone and took a picture of the license plate. Then I said to Johnny, "Apparently God has a plan for me, and He'll let me know when He's ready."

There was a boost to my confidence after seeing that license plate that God was indeed lining up my next project. My mind tried to fill in the details of what that might entail—perhaps to go back to work on the same cruise ship next April...? Although if that were the case, since it was only early November, what was I going to do until then? Uncertain of my future, I said goodbye to Johnny and drove home.

Two months later, I was getting a bit worried as my prayers to God had gone unanswered. I still had no idea what His plan was for me. However, I did receive an unexpected yet welcome call from my friend, Tina Miller. She invited me to be a guest on an upcoming episode of her TV show, "Open Up Live," in Bakersfield, California.

The day before joining her, I got a text message from Tina asking me to provide her producer, Spencer, some pictures of my recent Alaskan adventures. I emailed him several photos that I had taken of bears, glaciers, and breathtaking landscapes. Additionally, my mentor, David, had already designed a rough draft of this book's cover, so I sent Spencer a picture of that as well. I also emailed him the photograph that I took of the GODSPLN license plate.

In the final segment of my guest appearance with Tina, she asked Spencer to put the picture of my book's cover on the TV screen. For some reason, without being asked to, he had created a graphic that combined *both* the picture of the book cover and the photo of the GODSPLN license plate—even though I had sent them to him individually. Why would he do that?

Tina had told me that Spencer, a young twenty-something college student, was not her regular producer for the show, but that he was only filling in for that one episode.

When Spencer's graphic came on the screen—a mere three feet in front of my eyes—I was so focused on my interview with Tina that I didn't immediately realize its significance. A week later, however, while at home enjoying my morning meditation, I recalled that graphic on the screen. I *finally* realized the unmistakable message of what God's plan was for me. Seeing those two elements together— the book cover *and* the license plate—gave me the most direct and specific answer that I could ever expect to receive. *God's plan was for me to write this book.*

> *If any of you lacks wisdom, let him ask God,*
> *who gives to all liberally and without reproach,*
> *and it will be given to him. [NKJV Bible James 1:5]*

Shortly after finishing my meditation, I called Tina to tell her of my epiphany. She was elated that through Spencer's fortuitous graphic, God had answered my prayer by sending that clear and indisputable sign. That's why I chose to share the following stories in this book.

CHAPTER 1: A LIFE OF EVOLVING BELIEFS

W hen I sat down to begin writing this book, I was filled with great enthusiasm. There were so many phenomenal coincidences, or "God shots," that I'd experienced over the past eight years. I had to share them with someone. Although my faith is on more solid footing now, it was by no means always that way. It has been more a life of evolving beliefs which included a good share of battles with my demons...and with God.

I grew up in a small southern New England town. My first involvement with God came through my relationship with my great-grandmother, Mabel. She was heavily engrossed in her church in Vermont. I was around eight years old when I began recognizing her relationship with our Lord.

Whenever I visited Mabel, I enjoyed attending her church and the numerous events there. The potluck dinners were my favorite. It seemed like Mabel never missed any activity of significance at that church. Her passion for the Lord was a constant source of positive energy and focus, demonstrated by the way she lived her life. Consequently, it was impossible not to feel my own kind of happiness when I thought about Him.

Years later, when Mabel died, our family gift to her church was a new sign out front. It seemed to be the perfect remembrance of her. She always lived her life front and center for God.

Thanks to Mabel's example, when I was about ten years old, I became an acolyte at a local church. My duties included lighting the candles and doing other simple chores for the Sunday morning services. Even so, neither reading the Bible nor learning more about God had ever crossed my mind.

I continued to serve in that church for a couple of years before giving up my position there. Then I began to focus on what I perceived to be more important things, like playing little league baseball. I also had school, homework, baseball practice, and Boy Scouts. How could I possibly have time to go to church and serve God along with so many other extracurricular activities?

Not long after my final at-bat in little league, I began attending high school and eventually became part of a small group of like-minded students. We joined together with one of our teachers, Ken Grady, who guided us to start one of the first fifty FM radio stations in American high schools. Those efforts by Ken helped numerous students, including me, launch wonderful careers in both the broadcasting and entertainment businesses.

Through social media, I have been able to keep in contact with Ken and his wonderful wife, Jean. They're a continual source of inspiration for so many people around the country and beyond. Each week, they produce and host their multi-award-winning TV and internet show, "Gospel Music Today."

I enjoyed some nice successes during my broadcasting career. That's evidenced by the multiple honors that I'd received. They include winning two awards from the Associated Press for my work in radio news. During that time, I was blessed to cover events attended by three former U.S. presidents, Jimmy Carter, Gerald R. Ford, and George H. W. Bush. I was also a reporter for the CBS Radio

Network, the Associated Press Radio Network, and the all-news WEEI 590 AM in Boston.

Next, I became the executive producer and weekend host of the syndicated radio show "The Sports Final." It was broadcast nationally from a studio in Boston. This allowed me to cover significant sporting events, including Major League Baseball's World Series and professional golf tournaments. I also reported on Boston's top professional sports teams: Celtics basketball, Bruins hockey, Patriots football, and Red Sox baseball.

Like many young boys, I dreamed of one day playing professional sports. Although it turned out that wasn't my calling, I did have some tremendous experiences vicariously as a sports reporter. For instance, each time that I walked onto the field at Fenway Park—home of the Red Sox—I was able to stand at home plate and stare at the famed "Green Monster." (That's what they call the unusually high green wall and scoreboard combination in left field, which separates the playing field from the bleacher seats.) It was an almost indescribable feeling being on that field. The rich green grass was perfectly manicured. There was also an invigorating energy swirling throughout the ballpark. Even more, I could talk to the players as they waited to take batting practice.

Looking into the stands, I used to imagine what it must be like to play baseball in front of thousands of fans. That has to be an incredible feeling.

I also covered sporting events at the old Boston Garden. Before being torn down, it was one of the most iconic arenas in sports history. The Boston Celtics and the Los Angeles Lakers had some of their most famous basketball games there. They featured Larry Bird of the Celtics and Earvin "Magic" Johnson of the Lakers. Watching two such legends battle each other was almost beyond reality.

Those of us covering the New England Patriots were allowed to go onto the field and stand in the back of the end zone during the last five minutes of each game. This saved us from having to deal with the crowds leaving the stadium afterwards as we headed to the locker rooms to interview the players. Plus, it was another powerful experience. From up in the press box you have a great view of the game, but you cannot truly feel the intensity of the players' bodies colliding with each other on the field. Being near the end zone gave me a real appreciation for the physical ability that it takes to play professional football.

There were numerous other experiences that I had during my broadcasting career. They included being the Public and Media Relations Director for two professional sports teams. I also produced and hosted the Brown University football half-time show. In addition, I worked as an on-air personality at six radio stations in New England along with producing and hosting a weekly sports show on cable TV.

Unfortunately, as my career was progressing, I discovered new forms of entertainment. They definitely did not include God and eventually led me to excessive drinking and snorting cocaine.

One of my craziest days as a reporter occurred in 1987. I was scheduled to cover a Patriots game at their stadium in Foxborough, Massachusetts. The night before, I hung out with some friends and wound up drinking heavily and sniffing cocaine. Nonetheless, after not having slept for nearly twenty-four hours, I left my friend's apartment around eleven the next morning to go to the game, which began at one o'clock. Driving my car, it took me nearly an hour to get to the stadium; all the while, I continued to snort coke as I traveled on the freeway. Incredibly, I didn't cause an accident or hurt anyone. I did, however, do one last line of cocaine in my car when I arrived at the stadium.

Stumbling out of my sedan, I walked a couple of hundred yards and entered the press box elevator. Only two other people were in it—Hall of Fame quarterback Joe Namath and Hall of Fame broadcaster Pat Summerall. Stoned out of my mind, I felt amazingly trapped, like being in an overstuffed subway car during rush hour. I *so* wanted to get out and wait for the next elevator, but the door closed and up we went.

I'm not sure whether Joe or Pat noticed my hyped-up state of being, but neither one of them said anything to me. Surprisingly, rather than do my best to hide my state from them, I made a comment to Joe, telling him how people used to say I looked like a younger version of him. That was when my late grandfather, Homer, took my family to Army football games at West Point, New York. Joe responded kindly. Almost simultaneously, the elevator door to the press box opened. Thank God. Although the ride up took only a few seconds, it seemed like an eternity.

Making matters worse, I now had to sit side by side with all the other reporters. There was hardly any room for me to move in the small press area and the game would last for three hours. Having no more cocaine with me to help maintain my alertness made it quite challenging. I was ready to explode. Surely, that's not the way to report on a game.

Immediately after it ended, I had to go into the hot and sweat-filled Patriots locker room. In my wretched condition, it was definitely not the place for me to be, but I needed to get sound bites from the players for my national radio broadcast later that night. Then I had to drive forty-five minutes to the studio in Boston to produce and host the show. In anticipation, I'd left enough cocaine in my car to keep me awake during the ride and while I was on air. Afterwards, I was able to pass out on the couch in the studio.

Yes, I know—absolute insanity. Sadly, I could go on with many similar stories, but I trust that you've been able to get the picture. My life, lived on self-will, was hardly anything that you would call a success.

Eventually my career was put on hold as I became homeless. For several months, I slept on couches at friends' and family members' homes. Then one day, I hopped on a bus to live on the streets of Fort Lauderdale, Florida. While there, I nearly left this planet.

* * *

NEW LOCATION...SAME RESULTS

Although homeless, once I arrived in South Florida, I was able to continue my partying lifestyle. The day after I got there, I was fortunate to obtain a job as a bartender in a local pub. When my first night of work ended, I grabbed a tablecloth from the supply room so that I could use it to help keep me warm while I slept outside. Not far from the pub, there was a small apartment complex with a secured pool area. I walked there, hopped over the fence, and slept on a lounge chair. It was definitely not an ideal situation, but was much more comfortable and warmer than sleeping on the ground. This nightly journey continued for several weeks.

Four friends from New England had moved to Fort Lauderdale shortly before I did. One of them allowed me to leave my suitcase in the trunk of his car. I also kept a small duffle bag in a locker at the Greyhound bus station. Every morning, I walked about three miles from the pool area to get there. In the bathroom, I would shave, brush my teeth, and do my best to clean myself. Then I'd walk another couple of miles to the beach and get some more rest. Any food that I had was mostly from convenience stores (potato chips, doughnuts, sodas, etc.). It was not a lifestyle that I would recommend to anyone.

You may be wondering why my friends did not allow me to live with them. The answer is simple. They rented two very small cottages, with two guys and their girlfriends living in each one. There wasn't any room for me.

After a couple of months, though, one of my friends felt really sorry for me and let me move into his cottage and sleep on the small patch of floor space between his bed and the wall. That area was only about three feet wide, but it sure was nicer than being outside. Plus, I now had a shower to use as well, which saved me a daily trip to the bus station.

I slept on the cottage floor for a couple of months, and eventually I was able to rent my own apartment. While getting my own place might seem like a blessing, in fact, it simply allowed me to increase my partying without anyone else bothering me. So, rather than my life getting better, it was actually getting worse.

During the next few years in south Florida, I worked as a bartender for several different venues. On a regular basis, I poisoned myself with cocaine and alcohol. Not surprisingly, because of that, my thought process weighed heavily upon me. It brought me to a point where I felt that there was no need for me to continue living. Destitute, I believed that I only had one option: jumping off the bridge near the cruise ship terminal. My goal was to be struck dead by one of the large boats there—thus ending such a promising life.

Two weeks after having that thought, I was walking to my jumping-off point to end my life, when a voice came into my head— suggesting that I go out to Hollywood and try to make something of my life. That was definitely a strange experience because I wasn't someone who normally heard voices. Now confused as to what to do, I decided to turn around and go sit on Fort Lauderdale beach to ponder my future. Was this my first real encounter with God?

Through a series of events over the next several months, I ended up back in southern New England. The night after enjoying Thanksgiving with my family there, I went to visit my then girlfriend, Sherrie, at her home. We ended up in a lively conversation about how we should spend the night together. As our chat carried on, I definitely did not express any notion of being *thankful* for Sherrie's presence in my life. So, after about thirty minutes, I decided to leave her alone and head out on the town to go drinking by myself.

As the result, on November 28, 1992, at approximately two thirty in the morning, I was stopped by a police officer for erratic driving. The patrolman asked me to step out of the truck that I had borrowed from my friend, Steve, and then had me perform a series of physical tasks. I'm guessing that I didn't do too well as I was handcuffed, put in the back of a squad car, and driven to the police station. Once there, I flunked the breathalyzer test and was ticketed for DUI, after which I was put in a jail cell to sober up.

Nearly two hours later, at about four thirty in the morning, I was allowed to go home. Unfortunately, Steve's truck had already been towed away and locked up. I was definitely in no condition to be driving anyway. I needed to find a ride home.

Steve lived thirty minutes away and I was *not* about to call him. Thus, I phoned Sherrie, as she lived only a few miles from the police station. Understandably agitated by my call, she nevertheless agreed to come get me.

I anxiously waited for Sherrie in the station's lobby. Fifteen minutes later, she walked through the door. I can assure you that I was now extraordinarily *thankful* that Sherrie was in my life. At that point in time, it was often painful to see what I sometimes needed to go through in order to be grateful for many of the people and things in my life.

That said, as Sherrie came into the lobby, she stopped about twenty feet from me. Feeling completely defeated and ashamed, I looked at her and said, "I'm done." She replied, "I can smell you from here." That night was the last time that I've ever had an alcoholic drink.

* * *

GO WEST AND BEWARE

Eleven months later, I had nearly a year of sobriety and decided to follow that voice that I'd heard in my head back in Florida. It was time for me to move to the land of swimming pools and movie stars. Hollywood, here I come! My dad was generous enough to give me a car. I had a few dollars in my pocket, so off I went on my cross-country journey.

Driving mostly on southern highways, I spent the majority of my time traveling on Routes 40 and 10. About a week after I left southern New England, I arrived in Hollywood, knowing no one and with no place to live.

There was an ad in a local newspaper listing a room for rent in an apartment with a Christian woman. Figuring that she wasn't into drugs or excessive partying, I gave her a call. We had a good talk; however, she said that because I was a male, her religious beliefs would prohibit me from living with her. Regardless, she invited me to join her the next night at a church in a Los Angeles suburb. After our conversation, I rented a room in a cheap motel for the night.

The following evening, I ventured out to meet the woman at her church. About a month later, the pastor there dipped me in a giant pool of water as I turned my life over to Jesus and was born again. Seemingly, that was the beginning of my newfound relationship with God...but not quite so fast.

For several months, I attended numerous events at that church. One morning, I was in the overflow room watching a service on the big-screen TV. When it ended, I got up and grabbed my jacket. At the same time, the head pastor, who had just finished preaching, came walking down a short set of stairs towards me. He was dressed in a well-fitted suit and tie. His hair was thinning, but neatly groomed. This man was thought of very highly in the church community across the country.

Curiously, I had been near the pastor on several occasions without having any negative feelings—yet, that morning, for some unknown reason, my encounter with him was tremendously frightening. My eyes caught his and his eyes caught mine. Immediately, an intense feeling of horror went through me. I was absolutely freaked out. This was something that I'd never experienced before. I felt that if there truly was a devil on this planet, he was standing right in front of me.

The pastor had a scary dark look in his eyes. As he stared back at me, I felt like he knew that I was onto him. My thoughts were solidified when he quickly took a left-hand turn and walked swiftly down the hallway. His normal routine after the service was to spend time in the overflow room talking with churchgoers.

While the pastor headed away from me, I ran out of the church as fast as I could and continued for about a half-mile down the street to my car. I drove off completely shaken by what I had just experienced. That one encounter led me to turn my back on all churches for many years. After such a traumatic incident, God was definitely not at the top of my list of interests. I began pondering whether I would ever go back to a church. Without a doubt, it would take a miracle.

* * *

REPLACING A LEGEND

A few days after I had moved to California, I rented an apartment in Glendale, a bit north of downtown Los Angeles. To pay my bills, I took a job selling cars at a well-known dealership. I enjoyed some nice successes there, reflected in my winning several awards for my sales and customer service.

After a year and a half, however, I was looking for a new challenge and responded to a newspaper ad for an on-air host at a TV shopping network. Two weeks after I sent my resumé, I met with the management team there and, surprisingly, I was hired on the spot. That began a nearly fifteen-year career of producing and hosting live TV shopping shows. It was an industry that allowed me to excel by using several of the talents that God had given me, including a credible voice, creativity, customer relations, and leadership.

Ultimately, I wound up as the general manager at that network. A couple of years later, I moved on to become the executive producer at another such venue. In all, I was blessed to have worked at nine TV shopping networks—eight in California and one in Texas.

The most thrilling opportunity of my hosting career occurred after the sudden passing of Billy Mays, arguably the most well-known and prolific pitchman on television. There was a casting call for candidates aspiring to replace Billy as "America's Next Great Pitchman." A competition for that honor was being sponsored by the country's top infomercial company. It had received *thousands* of entries from across America, including my own. Eventually, the company owners narrowed their choices down to only twenty-five finalists—and I was one of them!

A couple weeks after being notified of their decision, I flew to New York for my audition which took place in a small studio not far from Times Square. On a closed-circuit TV in a separate room, I was able to watch the other contestants who performed before me. Most of them gave pretty standard pitches and were not very creative. Believing that the company was looking for someone unique, I chose to add some humor and flair to my script.

When it was time for me to audition, an assistant led me from the waiting room to the studio. The stage on which I would perform was a few feet higher than the judges who were sitting at a table directly in front of me. Among them were the company owner and his wife.

Throughout my performance, I was being videoed by a man with a handheld camera, who had the lens practically right in my face. In spite of that, I nailed my audition. Even so, I didn't know exactly what kind of pitchman the company was hoping to find. Walking back to my hotel room, I wondered how this opportunity might turn out. My answer would come much sooner than I expected.

A few hours after my performance, at about two o'clock in the afternoon, I was sitting in my hotel room near Times Square when my cellphone rang. It was a call from a representative of the infomercial company. She asked me if I could stay overnight in New York City to do a live repeat performance of my audition the next morning on the news program *Fox & Friends*. I replied that I would be thrilled to represent them on TV. I then spent the next several hours rehearsing my script before getting a good night's sleep.

The next morning at four thirty, one of the company associates picked me up at my hotel and drove me a few blocks to the Fox Studios. Once there, I was cleared by security and escorted into the "green room," where I grabbed a cup of coffee and a bagel, then sat with the owner of the infomercial company. Glancing at the studio monitor, I was surprised to see Dwayne Johnson, aka "The Rock," there promoting one of his movies in the segment before mine. It occurred to me that he was probably (unintentionally) building the audience for my appearance immediately afterward. Wow! (I had the good fortune to take a picture with him right before my presentation.)

If I recall correctly, I was escorted into the studio just after 7:30 a.m. It was time for me to step in front of the cameras. The hundreds of hours that I'd previously hosted shows on TV shopping networks would now prove quite valuable. Although surrounded by a studio full of strangers, I felt right at home. My thirty-second pitch went extremely well and I received accolades from the show's host, Brian Kilmeade, and numerous production personnel. The company owner then told Brian that I was now one of *four* finalists, and that I'd be put on-camera for a screen test.

When it was time to leave the studio, a car service drove me to LaGuardia airport. This brief, though spirited, New York trip had truly been a tremendous experience.

About a week after arriving back in Los Angeles, I received a call from one of the company representatives, who congratulated me for *winning* the pitchman contest! All my years of hard work and dedication to the TV shopping industry had seemingly paid off. I was elated, and eager to do my first infomercial, wondering how this would play into my future career.

Despite all the hoopla, however, nothing significant has yet materialized from my winning performance. Such is Hollywood.

* * *

SCENT OF A MIRACLE

On a warm and sunny Saturday afternoon, nearly ten years after arriving in Los Angeles, I attended a party at a friend's house. His large backyard was filled with about one hundred people, food, drinks, and a classic rock band. Looking for a place to sit, I found what I thought was the only available seat. A few minutes later, though, I'd be proven wrong.

That seat was on the other side of a small bench where my friend Eric was sitting. I sat down and, soon after, an attractive woman came over and stood in front of us. She introduced herself, and we all ended up in a conversation. Shortly afterward, the woman squeezed onto the bench between Eric and me. Her attention became focused solely on me and we continued talking. Eric got up and walked away. Before we knew it, a couple of hours had passed by, and the band was packing up its equipment. The woman and I were the only two people left in the backyard.

Now, I mentioned to you earlier that it would most likely take a *miracle* to once again get me to trust in God. Never could I have predicted what happened next.

The woman offered me her telephone number, and reached into her purse for something on which to write. Not able to find any paper, she pulled out a perfume sample card that she had picked up while shopping the day before. She wrote on the card and handed it to me. I was immediately struck with a sense of awe when I realized that she had written her name and phone number above the name of the perfume—*Miracle.*

The next day, I began dating the *Miracle* woman (who had a six-year-old son, Christopher, and an eight-month-old daughter, Sadie). Three years later, we were married. I went from my single life to having an instant family.

During our marriage, at my wife's urging, I eventually became involved in a new church. Not long afterward, I ended up overseeing their homeless ministry. Some amazing volunteers, including my wife and kids, helped me to expedite the growth of the Monday program. In a short time, we went from feeding about fifty people free lunches to serving nearly three hundred attendees every week.

One of the keys to our success was making the meal experience feel like a family event. Guests ate on banquet tables with flower centerpieces, while some of them entertained us by playing their guitars during lunch. A woman from a beauty school brought some of her students to give our transient visitors free haircuts. Church-goers donated money to help us provide our attendees with clothing and toiletries. We also had volunteers who offered free job assistance and legal help.

Before lunch each week, I shared a sermon—a mix of my recovery experiences and stories from the Bible. Also, I made sure that I hugged every person who joined us. Some wore clean clothes; others were not as fortunate. It didn't matter. The look in their eyes as we embraced was priceless. I felt tremendously blessed to have become friends with so many of those Monday guests.

Unfortunately, once the homeless ministry grew, the church and I had different thoughts on how to continue its expansion. Thus, I felt that it was best for me to step aside. Within two weeks of the church's takeover, I was called by one of the homeless gentlemen I'd gotten to know there. He told me that nearly half of the Monday guests had stopped attending the lunch festivities. That was very sad for me to hear. I strongly felt, though, that God was calling me onto my next assignment.

Now, with my renewed vigor for God, I created, produced, and hosted the worldwide internet radio show *In Your Face*. For more than three years, the show aired Monday through Friday on the former Indie104.com. *In Your Face* was tracked in ninety-nine countries and focused on miracles and testimonies of my daily guests.

Mark "Maverick" Coon owned the radio station. While I was hosting a show one day, he sent me a shocking text message. Mark claimed that there were more than one-and-a-half-million people logged on to the Indie104.com website and that our server almost crashed. I was blown away; how could that be? The only advertising that I had was God. There were a few other occasions where Mark sent me similar texts.

In addition to *In Your Face*, I was inspired to write my first God-themed book. It was titled *God, Bless America...Before It's Too Late*. As you can see, I was apparently "all in" working for God, yet I still didn't have the intimate relationship with Him that I have today.

* * *

FAMILY TIME

The other significant part of my life at this time was being a husband and a father—which was tremendously rewarding. I enjoyed watching both Christopher and Sadie along with my wife as they participated in numerous school and community activities. Having been sober many years, I helped my wife organize the Red-Ribbon Week anti-drug program, an annual event that took place at our kids' elementary school.

My first year being involved with that program was very gratifying. Some of our local policemen and firemen joined us and gave the students hands-on experience with their vehicles. Plus, I was able to contact Lil' Zane, an actor and singer who starred in a Disney Channel show. He graciously volunteered to come out and entertain the students at their assembly. Unexpectedly—although very much appreciated—Lil' Zane didn't just sing a few songs; he also visited classrooms, signed autographs, and took pictures, making it a very exciting day at the school.

Another wonderful experience that I had was watching my son Christopher's first-ever Little League baseball championship game. His team was the Pirates; their opponents were the Dodgers. With the scored tied 2 to 2 in the bottom of the sixth inning, Christopher was the first batter for the Pirates. As the pitcher hurled the ball his way, he belted it over the centerfielder's head. Jumping to their feet, the ecstatic crowd of about one hundred people screamed with excitement as Christopher raced his way to second base for a lead-off double.

Christopher wasn't the fastest player on the Pirates, so the coach sent in a runner to replace him—as he had accomplished exactly what his team needed. Two batters later, the runner would score what proved to be the winning run. The Pirates held on to beat the Dodgers 3 to 2.

When the game ended, Christopher was mobbed on the field by his teammates. He was then given the game ball, which had been signed by all of the Pirates players and coaches, making this a memory he would surely never forget.

My daughter Sadie decided that she wanted to get involved in mixed league basketball. During her first year, Sadie had to compete with teammates who had much more experience than her. That was challenging, though, as the boys on her team didn't include Sadie in many of the plays. They rarely passed the ball to her even though she worked just as hard as they did during practice.

One Saturday afternoon, however, I snuck out of work and was able to see Sadie score her first-ever basket. It was in the last game of the season and her team was down by six points with only a couple of minutes left on the clock. Sadie was standing alone at the top of the foul circle where she finally received a crucial pass from one of the boys. She bounced the ball once, glanced around her and saw that she was all by herself. Sadie then heaved the ball exactly as she'd been practicing and banked it off the backboard into the basket. That shot kicked off the comeback that ultimately won the game and sent her team into the playoffs the following week—where they eventually won the championship. Sadie now had an extraordinary memory that she'll always remember.

For me, it was a great thrill to have watched both Christopher and Sadie enjoy some early life successes. Their stories, along with the others recounted in this chapter, always bring back many wonderful yet somewhat painful memories for me.

As I think about the experiences I'm about to describe, I am filled with similar feelings. However, these upcoming stories take an added dimension as they are filled with what I believe are truly improbable and (in many cases) mind-boggling coincidences.

CHAPTER 2: THOU SHALT NOT STEAL

This first "coincidental" story began with a chance meeting between my now ex-wife and three strangers. While attending a local fair one evening, a middle-aged man and woman and a twelve-year-old boy named Anthony crossed paths with my wife. They began conversing and the four of them had a wonderful chat.

Later that evening, my wife told me about their conversation. The man and woman with Anthony were family friends who were temporarily caring for him. They disclosed that Anthony was currently up for adoption because his parents were strung out on drugs and living in sordid conditions. It was a sad story to hear, yet my wife caught me completely off-guard when she told me that we needed to make Anthony a part of our family. I had to pause for a moment to take in what I just heard. I mean, I wasn't necessarily against the idea; it just took me by surprise. We did have an extra bedroom in our house, so there would be room for him. My wife and I went on to discuss this together for some time as it was an important matter to consider. Accordingly, before I went to bed, I prayed to God for guidance about the proposition at hand.

The next day, I agreed to see if we would qualify to be Anthony's new parents. My wife then contacted Child Services to let them know of our wish. Thus began a lengthy series of interviews, background checks, and court sessions. About two months into the process, we were granted the right to have Anthony move into our home. He instantaneously became a member of our family, fitting in nicely with our other two children. Sadie was now eight years old, and Christopher was fourteen years old.

Anthony had Asperger syndrome, a high-functioning form of autism. He was as smart as anyone could be, but he also had temper issues. His counselor told us that Anthony had built-up frustrations, apparently from dealing with his challenging situation with his biological parents, especially his mother. Even so, a few months after moving into our home, Anthony was well immersed in our family.

My wife and I were getting close to signing Anthony's final adoption papers. Then, one afternoon, I got an unexpected and disturbing telephone call from her. She said that Anthony had taken a swing at Sadie while the two of them were in the back seat of my wife's car. This was very disheartening, as I had to protect Sadie, but I also cared greatly about Anthony's well-being.

When I got home later that evening, I brought the two of them together in Sadie's room to discuss the situation. Neither had much to say. Anthony seemed more confused than sorry, although he did express some regret. As for Sadie, she seemed like she didn't want to say anything that would get Anthony in trouble. It also appeared to me that, whatever might have happened, she had already moved beyond the incident. I wondered if my wife had over-reacted and made more of the situation than was really there.

Since it was getting towards their bed time, and I was exhausted from a long day of work, I didn't probe any deeper. Rather, I gave Anthony and Sadie each a hug and told them that I loved them.

Next, I went to see my wife and share with her my conversation with the kids. I told her that I didn't get much from them, and that they did not seem too concerned about what may have happened that afternoon. My wife, however, made it clear to me that she was worried about Anthony's behavior. She reiterated her claim that he had taken a swing at Sadie, and wanted us to ensure her safety. I respected my wife's feelings even while I was uncertain of the exact circumstances surrounding the incident. Kids will be kids, and at this point I felt that the matter was resolved.

Three days later, on Sunday, Anthony attended services with our family at Christ's Church of the Valley in San Dimas, California. As he had done for several months, Anthony sat in the front row with the four of us, joining in as we sang and worshipped. Our pastor, Jeff, had set up a small inflatable pool of water just off to the side of where were sitting. It was used for baptisms for people who wanted to become *born again*, which they could do at the end of each service.

Anthony had watched parishioners of all ages take part in these ceremonies for many weeks. While doing so this Sunday, he looked at me and said, "Dad, next week I want to do that." I told him that it was a personal choice, something that he had to do for himself and not because he thought it would make my wife and me happy. He responded, "No Dad, I want to do it for me."

"Let the little children come to Me, and do not forbid them; for of such is the Kingdom of God. Assuredly, I say to you, whoever does not receive the kingdom of God as a little child will by no means enter it." [NKJV Bible Mark 10: 14-15]

The following Sunday, my wife, the three kids, and I all dressed up for Anthony's big day. Arriving at the church, we sat in the front row as usual. About ninety minutes later, the service was ending. Pastor Jeff called for anyone looking to give his/her life to Jesus to come forward. Anthony stood up and said, "I'm gonna do it, Dad." I looked at him and patted him on the back.

He then walked over and talked privately with one of the prayer counselors. I'm not sure exactly what they discussed, but the next thing I knew, Anthony was being dunked in the pool of water. He was born again. Soaked from head to toe, Anthony stepped out of the pool brimming with excitement. The look of accomplishment on his face was priceless. I couldn't have been more proud of him.

Just over two weeks later, though, my wife called me to complain once again about Anthony's behavior, saying that he had pushed Sadie as they were playing in her room. Hearing those words really sent a dagger through my heart, as I couldn't believe what my wife was telling me. If it were true, then clearly I could not allow Sadie to get injured because of Anthony's actions. However, I was truly caught off-guard, as this was not the Anthony that I'd grown to know over the past several months. I was in shock and needed to quickly figure out the best way to handle this situation. Unfortunately, that day I had to work extra-long hours and everyone was asleep by the time I got home. So I didn't get the opportunity to discuss the matter with anyone.

As it happened, I never would have the chance.

Before I woke up the next morning, my wife apparently had some personal business that she needed to tend to. On her way there, she dropped off Christopher and Sadie at school. For some reason, Anthony had no school that day. It also happened to be my day off from work.

While my wife was out running errands, she phoned one of the counselors at Child Services to report her claims of Anthony's recent behavior. I'm not exactly sure what transpired during that conversation but, afterward, my wife called to inform me that we needed to bring Anthony back to the State the following morning and call off the adoption. I was completely shocked by what she told me, and absolutely floored by what she said. This couldn't be happening....

It took several moments to sink in. I always thought that my wife and I had fairly good communication, so when she didn't include me in a call of such significance, I was really surprised. Once the shock wave passed, though, I couldn't bear the thought of Anthony not becoming an official part of our family as we had eagerly anticipated. We were only one court hearing away from his adoption.

Distraught, after about an hour of processing this whole situation, I called my wife to see if there was any other option than canceling the adoption. After all, we had endured numerous months of waiting, attending interviews, along with multiple background checks and court hearings in our efforts to clear the way for Anthony to *officially* become part of our family. Plus, from the first day he arrived in our home, Anthony had blended in well with all four of us. I had grown to love him and had been acting as if he was already my son.

Nevertheless, during our phone conversation, my wife indicated that Anthony's counselor was insistent that we bring him back to her the following morning. Without my input, the decision had already been made—and I felt angry and completely helpless. My heart sank in my chest.

What especially bothered me was knowing that Anthony was such a great kid with a big, loving heart and an enthusiastic outlook on life. Oddly, for one who supposedly had temper issues, they never really manifested themselves—at least not to me.

Even now, several years later, I still wonder what, if anything, actually transpired between Anthony and Sadie on those two occasions.

* * *

HEARTBREAKING NEWS

Still reeling from that fateful phone call from my wife, I was home by myself, left with the daunting task of delivering the heartbreaking news to Anthony.

After the call with my wife ended, I decided that Anthony should have a memorable day of fun before going back to Child Services. I was unsure of where he'd be placed. Anthony might be stuck in a home where he wasn't able to enjoy extracurricular activities. That would be extremely disheartening. He was such an energetic and active young man.

Putting my phone down, I went to visit Anthony in his bedroom, although I felt that now was surely not the time for me to tell him the sad news. I needed to think about the best way to handle the situation. I asked Anthony to name three places that he always wanted to go to but had never been. He responded with Disneyland, miniature golfing, and go-cart racing. Jackpot! There was a small theme park about thirty minutes away in Ontario, California, that had miniature golfing and go-cart rides. We'd go there and have a fun—though agonizing—last day together.

That said, before Anthony and I ventured into our afternoon, we needed to eat some lunch. I knew just the right place—the Rainforest Cafe, which has an awesome atmosphere and great food for kids. So off we went. I can't recall our conversation as I drove nearly a half an hour to the restaurant, but I remember that it was extremely challenging for me to hold back my tears.

Upon arriving at the eatery, Anthony lit up with excitement. He had me take a picture of him with the large alligator replica out front. Inside, he enjoyed a burger, fries, and a fruit smoothie drink. The restaurant's energetic atmosphere of thundering noises, water falling, and animal replicas kept us entertained. Granted, it was tormenting for me to talk with Anthony as we ate and pretend that nothing was wrong. About thirty minutes after we began eating, it was time for some fun, although I was still dreading the disappointing news that I had to break to him.

Leaving the restaurant, we hopped into my car for the quick ten-minute ride to the theme park. Arriving there, I was focused on pulling into the south side of the parking lot, where there were no cars. At the last minute, I decided to drive into the north side. When I parked, I noted that the vehicle in front of me had a cross on its back window. Exiting my car, I also saw a cross on the back window of the pickup truck behind us. Curiously, I noticed the words FAITH, HOPE & LOVE on the rear window of yet another nearby car.

With Anthony standing next to me, I realized that this was now the time that I needed to break the sad news to him. It was going to be one of the hardest things that I had ever done. So, while looking at Anthony, I silently prayed to God asking for guidance on this task.

Then I questioned Anthony about what he saw on the SUV in front of me. He replied, "A Cross." Next, I asked him the same thing concerning the other two vehicles behind us. He answered, "A cross and Faith, Hope and Love." I then asked Anthony what he thought that meant. His response was, "God is with us."

Now, I began scrambling for words to tell Anthony of his pending return to Child Services. I started by reminding him that God was with us. Continuing on, I said that—even so—it doesn't mean that things will always go our way. I brought up the two incidents where he had been supposedly aggressive towards Sadie. Anthony half-heartedly claimed to remember them but seemed not to recall whether or why he acted that way. I explained that, because of those incidents, his counselor had made a very tough decision: that we had to take him back to her the next morning.

As expected, Anthony reacted with shock and disbelief—sobbing and repeatedly asking why this was happening. It was tremendously heartbreaking for me as well. I let him express his feelings for several minutes, and then I hugged him and tried to bring him some sense of comfort. He was a twelve-year-old boy who had just had his hopes crushed. Anthony believed that he'd finally found a loving home with a family that adored him. The fact is that he did. Apparently, though, God had other plans for him.

With Anthony now calm, it was time for us to head into the small amusement park to play some miniature golf and go on a few rides. Walking to the window to pay our entrance fee, there was a nickel on the ground. Anthony picked it up. I asked him what it said on the front of it. He replied, "In God We Trust."

"Whenever I am afraid,
I will trust in You."
[NKJV Bible Psalm 56:3]

After buying our tickets, Anthony and I went inside and enjoyed a wonderfully fun round of miniature golf. (Anthony won.) Then he wanted to ride the go-carts. They had just opened the track and there was no waiting line. We had a blast racing against each other. For a first-timer, Anthony handled his go-cart quite well. I never could pass by him. When our rides ended, he wanted to go again. Although a short line had formed, we were able to quickly move to the front. Our second excursion around the race course was equally exhilarating.

The price of admission included unlimited miniature golf and our choice of any three rides. Anthony wanted to race the go-carts a third time. Now, however, the line was quite long and we'd have a fairly lengthy wait before our next turn.

Off to my left, I noticed a pool of water in which there were motorized inner tubes with large squirt guns attached to them. Thus, I told Anthony that he'd probably have more fun getting me wet rather than waiting in line again for the go-carts. Agreeing with my suggestion, Anthony walked with me over to the pool.

* * *

IN GOD WE TRUST

As soon as Anthony and I joined the line to the inner tubes ride, I noticed three shiny pennies on the ground. They were all facing heads-up and were only a few inches away from both us and the pool. I urged Anthony to grab them, which he did. Then I asked him what it said on the front of the pennies. He responded, "In God We Trust."

Next I asked Anthony where he found them. He said, "Near the water." I told him that he was right, and then I quizzed him on what he would call that body of water. "A pool," he answered.

"Correct," I replied. "And what did you do in the pool at our church a couple of weeks ago?" I asked him.

"I gave my life to Jesus," he answered.

"Exactly," I said. Continuing, I went on to explain my observations to Anthony.

Going back to Child Services was surely not what Anthony wanted. God, however, was letting him know that He had a wonderful plan for his life. I shared that as challenging as it may be, he needed to fully trust God. Anthony seemed to accept that thought process quite well.

It was now our turn to get on the inner tubes. Anthony proceeded to water me down with the giant squirt gun. I managed to soak him as well. We both had a blast on that ride. When it was over, Anthony wanted to play some more miniature golf. So we went to the customer service counter, grabbed our putters and golf balls, and proceeded to the first hole.

Anthony lined up his shot and hit his ball. Somehow, it took an extremely crazy bounce and we had no idea where it landed. By now, I'd used up all of my energy, trying to make sure that Anthony and I had a great last day together. Therefore, rather than go and get another ball for him, I gave him mine. I'd watch as he enjoyed playing out the round. This would prove to bring about another unexpected but amazing experience.

When Anthony finished the seventeenth hole, I picked up his ball and told him to put it in his pocket. That's because you only get one shot on the eighteenth hole. Even if you get a hole-in-one and win a free game, you can't retrieve your ball as it gets trapped behind a screen. Not knowing what life would be like for Anthony after that day, I wanted him to have a souvenir to remember our last time together.

Anthony's response to my request to pocket the ball caught me completely off guard. "No, Dad, that's stealing."

Say what? I thought, *Who is this kid?*

"Just go ahead and do it," I replied. "I want you to have a souvenir from our last day together."

Again, Anthony stood strong on his morals and echoed, "No, Dad, I can't. The Bible specifically says 'Thou Shalt Not Steal.'"

Bam! Right to my heart. Anthony hit me with one of God's Ten Commandments. How could I continue to debate him? I could not. My twelve-year-old son had me.

"Train up a child in the way he should go,
And when he is old he will not depart from it."
[NKJV Bible Proverbs 22:6]

---

* * *

SORRY HOLLYWOOD, GOD'S SCRIPT IS BETTER

Standing at the seventeenth hole, I felt totally defeated by Anthony's wisdom and morals. What could I do to end this day with a meaningful memory for him? The answer was simple. I didn't have to do anything. Anthony looked at me and said, "Don't worry, Dad, I'm gonna get a hole-in-one anyway and win a free game. Make sure you have your video on." We then made the short walk to the eighteenth hole.

For Anthony to get a hole-in-one, he'd have to hit his golf ball up a short hill at exactly the precise speed and accuracy. The hole at the top was just barely big enough to fit the ball. If he missed there would be no second shot. A screen prohibiting us from retrieving his ball was in front of the hole. The odds were definitely not in his favor.

Anthony wished for me to video his attempt. Unfortunately, when it comes to my cellphone, I'm truly not adept at using its many features. That said, I couldn't find its video recorder in time to capture the moment. Assuming that I was recording him, Anthony lined up his shot and hit the ball. All of a sudden, I heard bells and other noises. Anthony began jumping up and down and screaming. "I did it, Dad, I did it; I got a hole-in-one!" he shouted. Although there would be no video for Anthony to remember that moment, I did snap a picture of him holding the ticket for the free game that he won. Incredible!

I had done my best to help Anthony have a meaningful memory of our last day together—but he refused to pocket his golf ball at my request. As a result, God seemingly rewarded Anthony for not stealing the ball and honoring Him.

See, it doesn't matter what happens to the scorecard that Anthony kept from our round of miniature golf. He could even lose the ticket for the free game. Anthony now has something much more meaningful—the incredible memory of making that hole in one. No one can ever take that away from him.

Now it was nearly six o'clock, and Anthony and I were starving. I drove us home to pick up the rest of our family for dinner, but neither Christopher nor my wife were able to join us. Consequently, only Anthony, Sadie, and I enjoyed one last meal together. Chicken tenders were our choice at *Chic-fil-A*.

After we finished eating, it was time to head home. We'd have one last night to enjoy Anthony's company as part of our family. In the morning, he'd be going back to Child Services. That was definitely not something that I wanted to think about anymore.

Arriving at our house, Anthony, Sadie, and I were joined by my wife and Christopher. We all sat in the living room with each other, but said little during our time together. It was truly a very somber atmosphere. I was completely exhausted from our very emotional day together. After about an hour, I was unable to keep my eyes open any longer, so I gave Anthony a hug goodnight and headed to bed.

Before they went to school the following morning, Christopher and Sadie said their good-byes to Anthony. Then he, my wife, and I got in the car to drive to the counselor's office. The weather was cold, cloudy, and drizzly, so we had to fight the rush-hour traffic on slick Los Angeles freeways. It took us about ninety minutes to get there, twice as long as usual. That entire time, I kept wondering where Anthony would end up living. No doubt it was one of the worst feelings that I ever had. I didn't want to let him go. I prayed that he wouldn't be placed in a group home, but rather somewhere he'd be loved and appreciated for being such an amazing young man.

Arriving at the Child Services building, my wife, Anthony, and I, all walked inside. The atmosphere was anything but welcoming. There was a high ceiling, cement brick walls, a tile floor, and hard plastic seats. I believe that everything was a dark brown color. The three of us sat nervously waiting for Anthony's counselor to come out to get him. Talk about a heartbreaking several minutes.

When the counselor arrived, it was tears all around. My wife said her good-bye's first. Then it was my turn. While hugging Anthony, the thought of letting him go was emotionally wrenching, but the choice was not mine. Watching him walk off into another room with his counselor was even harder—especially as his next placement was still unknown.

The following day, however, my wife told me that she spoke to Anthony's counselor and received some great news. A single woman agreed to move Anthony into her home in a middle-class Los Angeles suburb. I was elated. Anthony had issues that he needed to deal with concerning his biological mother. Now he'd be living with a caring woman—one whom I expect would give him the love and attention that he deserved and needed. What a blessing!

As I look back over the events that I've shared in this chapter, I have to stop and think. There were numerous circumstances and perfectly aligned situations that created this story.

Here was Anthony, this wonderful twelve-year-old boy, up for adoption because his biological parents were incapable of caring for him due to their demons. Then, after a chance meeting with my wife, he eventually moved in with our family and believed that he had finally found the loving home he always wanted. Following his heart,

Anthony subsequently gave his life to Jesus. Shortly afterwards, he felt the tremendous pain of learning he could no longer live with us. Nevertheless, Anthony firmly trusted that God would still take care of him.

Even more, Anthony refused to follow my lead to put the golf ball in his pocket. Instead, Anthony demonstrated the immense respect he had for God's law. As a result, he was doubly rewarded. Not only does Anthony have the incredible memory of making that hole-in-one, but he was also gifted with what appears to be a secure home with a loving caregiver.

All in all, it would seem to be the perfect ending to a challenging story. Hollywood truly could not have written a better script.

CHAPTER 3: MESSAGE IN THE SAND

S ome blessings aren't meant to be "forever blessings." That's one of the aspects of life that I was reminded of from my experience in dealing with Anthony's adoption process.

I'd been married for just over six years when my wife and I had to return Anthony to Child Services. Shortly afterwards, I started seeing signs that perhaps his life wouldn't be the only one that would be heading in a different direction.

On a steady basis, numerous "coincidental signs" began coming across my path. After witnessing them for nearly a year, I became completely overwhelmed with the feeling that God had a different plan for my life. So, albeit extremely sad, I felt that it was best for me to end my marriage. Accordingly, in the middle of March, I went to live with my best friend, Johnny. He had a condo near Universal Studios Hollywood.

My parents suggested that I leave everything in the house with my wife and kids, except for my personal belongings, and trust that God would take care of me. Therefore, I left with the money in my pocket, some pictures, my clothes, and a computer.

In November, eight months after I'd filed for divorce, it had not yet been finalized. It was time, however, for me to visit my immediate family for the Thanksgiving holiday. Thus, I traveled from Los Angeles to New England to enjoy the festive occasion with them. We had a wonderful time at my mother's home sharing memories while eating some tasty turkey, mashed potatoes, and pumpkin pie.

After our meal, I stepped outside into the crisp autumn air to have a quick word with God. I told Him that I was going to go to the beach the next day to have an intimate talk with Him. There were some questions that I was hoping to have answered. Most importantly, I wanted to know from God whether or not I should make one last attempt to save my marriage.

The following day was sunny and not too chilly—a perfect fall day. About mid-afternoon, I began my nearly one-hour drive to the beach. I stopped at a store on the way and bought several boxes of crackers to feed the seagulls.

Upon arriving at the beach, I was greeted by a brisk, cool breeze as the sun generously glistened off the clear blue ocean. Walking to the edge of the water, I tossed some crackers to the only two seagulls there. Within seconds I was surrounded by at least thirty more of them. That was exciting.

As I enjoyed feeding my new friends, however, the daylight began to disappear around us. So I decided not to walk the beach as I had originally planned. My conversation with God would have to wait a bit longer. I told Him that I'd soon go to a nearby restaurant, order a bowl of chowder, and eat it in my car where, at last, I'd finally have my talk with Him.

Only one hour had passed since I began feeding the seagulls. Yet the sun had now set and a half-moon shined brightly above me. Finally, all the crackers had been eaten. Reluctantly, I said goodbye to my wonderful feathered friends. It was now time to have a conversation with God.

I was standing due south facing the ocean, which was about five feet in front of me. My car was parked off to the east nearly a hundred yards away. To my immediate right was a breakwall of large rocks. This was a barrier holding back the beach sand from the water, which allowed boats to travel through a channel from the docks to the ocean. About twenty-five yards behind me to the north was a closed snack stand.

While feeding the seagulls, I was so enthralled with them that I never looked behind me. Now, rather than heading east towards my car, I turned around. I'm not sure why. All of a sudden, I was taken aback and overwhelmed by what I saw and nearly fell to my knees in disbelief. Written in the sand, in letters each about three feet long, was the phrase, *I LOVE YOU.* The security light from the snack stand provided just enough brightness to make the message visible. Tears began to fill my eyes. I could not believe what I was seeing.

After staring at those words for several minutes, I wanted to take a picture of them to show everyone my miraculous find. Needing more light, I ran to my car and drove four miles to a store. I bought a flashlight and batteries, then raced back to the message in the sand. With my cellphone, I took numerous snapshots of it. What a phenomenal experience. How did that message end up there?

Tears flowed from my eyes, as I walked a short distance to the restaurant and finally got my bowl of chowder. Now, though, I was too emotionally drained to have my talk with God, but I wasn't all that disappointed. With great confidence, I felt that He had already shown me all that I needed to know in that perfectly written message in the sand—I LOVE YOU.

Surprisingly, that's not the end of this story. As part of my daily ritual, I do some spiritual reading. The day after visiting the beach, I was studying my Bible in the Book of Mark. In chapter 14, verse 28, it tells us that Jesus had been talking to His disciples and said to them:

"But after I have been raised, I will go before you to Galilee." [NKJV]

(Galilee was where Jesus delivered His Sermon on the Mount to the multitudes and His disciples.)

While reading that scripture, again my eyes began to fill with tears as I realized that where I saw the I LOVE YOU in the sand the day before was at *Galilee State Beach*. Incredible! There were several other beaches closer to me but, for some reason, I ended up going there.

I had told God that I was going to meet Him at a beach to ask Him whether or not I ought to make one last attempt to save my marriage. Apparently, He (or one of His angels) went there before me to leave me that message in the sand.

Indeed, that wasn't the specific answer from God that I wanted in regard to my marriage; however, seeing that message led me to believe that He was intimately watching over me. That, in turn, brought me immense peace that my life was headed in the right direction.

Nearly a month later, the day before Christmas, my divorce was finalized. Although I was sad at the outcome, I had more confidence in my decision to leave my wife after having seen that message on the beach—I LOVE YOU.

* * *

BUT WAIT...THERE'S MORE!

In March, four months after I had that incredible experience on Galilee State Beach, I was back in Los Angeles where I went to a twelve-step meeting. I shared with the group that—when I prayed—

I was not getting answers from God as to what direction I should focus concerning future employment opportunities.

Immediately after the meeting, I was pulled aside by my friend, Fred. He reminded me of our eleventh step from the book *Alcoholics Anonymous*. It reads:

> *[We] sought through prayer and meditation to improve our conscious contact with God as we understood Him, praying only for knowledge of His will for us and the power to carry that out.*

Fred said that I needed to not only pray but to meditate. That would allow my mind to be clear enough for God to share some of his wisdom with me. After finishing my conversation with Fred, I went directly home and laid quietly on the couch. Then I asked God for some insight into what my future career might look like. Before hearing an answer, though, I fell asleep.

However, three days later, during my new daily meditation routine, I got an inspiration to look online at one of the Hollywood casting websites. There I found an ad describing an intriguing employment opportunity from a company looking for a jewelry salesman in Juneau, Alaska.

The position came with a place to live, the use of a car, a salary, commission, and round-trip airfare from Los Angeles. It seemed too good to be true, but with my nearly fifteen years of experience (having sold jewelry on TV), I needed to at least send in my resumé.

Several days after doing so, I had the first of two online interviews with a company representative. As we were nearing the end of the second one, I was told that I was hired. Jackpot! My new job would begin the first week of May and would be the prelude to an incredible new chapter in my life.

Now, before heading to an unfamiliar territory, I wanted to get more information about that jewelry company. Its website showed that it was headquartered about two hours from where I lived; so I decided to drive there. Maybe I could meet some of the employees or possibly the owner. Any information that I might be able to gather could help me when I arrived in Juneau.

My red-flag alert was raised immediately upon reaching the company's storefront about eleven o'clock one weekday morning. Looking in the windows, I saw no one in the showroom and the display cases were empty. Walking around to the side of the older brick building, I saw a note for delivery drivers taped to a door, so I knocked. A few seconds later, a twenty-something man appeared and I asked him if I could speak with the owner. He told me to wait there and closed the door.

Shortly after, a gentleman, whom I'll call Mike, came outside. Introducing himself as the owner, he said that he recognized me from reviewing my online interviews. We chatted for a few moments. Mike mentioned that normally he doesn't hire someone with my experience. *Say what?* I was caught off guard by his statement and found it to be quite peculiar. You would think that an employee with vast knowledge and skills would be an asset to his company. This is especially true when you're dealing with the short Alaskan tourist season; you only have a few months to make a year's pay. Nonetheless, after our conversation, I went home and started preparing to go to Alaska for the first time in my life.

Once in Juneau, I was soon enlightened about the reality of this too-good-to-be-true opportunity. It was easy to see why Mike usually didn't hire someone with lots of experience in the jewelry business. The promises that he had made regarding possible financial compensation were not going to be achievable. That was a disappointing discovery.

Not surprisingly, about a month into this new employment venture, I was definitely not having any fun. After speaking with Steve, a company representative, we decided to part ways.

However, along with my job, I also lost my place to live and the use of the car. Thus, I told Steve that I'd need four days to move out. He agreed with my request. I just picked that number at random to give me time to make some decisions. There I was in a city that I had never been to with nowhere to live. Plus, my friend Johnny, with whom I'd been staying in Los Angeles, was selling his condo. So going back there was not an option. What could I do? I believe they call my predicament "being stuck between a rock and a hard place."

I had become involved in a twelve-step recovery program while in Juneau. The day after I talked to Steve, I shared about my situation at a meeting. A woman there, Ericka, said that she had an available room in her house that I could use at no charge. She also expressed that during normal business hours I'd be able to use her car. Unbelievable! Ericka stated that my staying in Juneau would be valuable to assisting others with their sobriety. I'd been sober for more than twenty years at that time. Realizing how incredible Ericka's offer was, I decided to accept her generosity and stay in Alaska.

Still needing a job, after the meeting, I prayed to God asking Him for specific direction. Was I definitely supposed to stay in Juneau? Or should I head back to Los Angeles? One more time, the day after I prayed, I got my answer.

Not only was I offered a nice employment opportunity in Juneau, but Ericka drove me to the Mendenhall Glacier. We were going to walk to the Nugget Falls waterfall. A sign indicated that getting there would be a one-mile hike on a designated trail. Looking around the area, I noticed that we could probably leap over the small stream in front of us and cut our walk in half by going our own route. Ericka agreed to the plan, so we jumped.

As Ericka and I landed across the stream and took three more steps, I immediately gasped, "You've gotta be kidding!" Ericka asked me what was wrong. There was nothing wrong, just another stunning message. Written in the sand directly in front of us was:

"I ♥ U." Not knowing that this "message" would be there, I had chosen this spot to jump over the stream.

Pulling out my cellphone, I showed Ericka the picture of the I LOVE YOU message that I had taken six months prior in the sand on Galilee State Beach. I then shared that story with her. She was as amazed as I was.

In only a matter of months, I had asked God twice for answers to questions concerning my well-being. Incredibly, both times (and thousands of miles apart), I received the same answer written in the sand—I LOVE YOU. Apparently, that's all God needed me to know.

Those messages were seemingly two powerful coincidences. However, as I was near the end of writing this story, I decided to look something up in the NKJV Bible. Thumbing through the pages, I happened to come across its definition of a miracle:

> *A miracle is an event that exceeds the known laws of nature and science, usually an act of God done through human agents.*

Presumably, humans had written those messages in the sand, yet after reading that definition, I had an intriguing thought. What kind of odds do you think Vegas oddsmakers would give me if I told them I was to pray to God and then find my answers clearly written in the sand? If they took that bet, imaginably, I would never have to work again.

CHAPTER 4: I WAS PRAYING...GOD WAS LISTENING

Staying at Ericka's house in Juneau during the summer was fantastic. She lived only two miles from my favorite place, the Mendenhall Glacier. The surrounding area is filled with stunning landscapes and numerous wildlife species, including black bears, bald eagles, beavers, porcupines, and so many different types of birds. It's one of the most relaxing, yet invigorating, places I have ever visited.

When winter came, though, so did the cold weather, along with short and dark days. My excitement for Juneau was not the same as it was in the summer. Therefore, I decided to spend some time back in the lower 48—what Alaskans call the mainland United States. My plan was to leave in early February and go back to Juneau in April, with the next tourist season beginning in May. I had already been asked to return to work for the tour company I'd worked for during the last season.

Before flying to Alaska the past summer, I left my car with my aunt and uncle in Arizona, so I needed to go back there to retrieve it. I called my aunt and shared my plan to visit them on the weekend of

February 7. Unfortunately, she said that she'd be out of town, so I scheduled my flight for the middle of the next week. That would allow me time to take care of some personal business and then hang out with my family on the weekend.

Arriving in Arizona on Wednesday night, February 11, I spent most of the next two days running errands. I had planned to spend time with my aunt and uncle on Saturday, but late Friday afternoon, I realized the next day was Valentine's Day. Not wanting to intrude upon them on such a special occasion, I decided to make other arrangements.

My original plan had been to leave for Los Angeles on Monday. I now decided that I would head out on Saturday morning. Consequently, I called my friend Everett in Rancho Mirage, California, which is about thirty minutes east of Palm Springs. I was scheduled to visit him on Monday afternoon. Now, however, I told Everett that I'd come by on Saturday and stay the night at his home. Sunday morning, I would continue the final three hours of my journey to Los Angeles.

During our conversation, Everett suggested going to Palm Springs—a very popular place for people to celebrate Valentine's Day—but then hesitated as he considered the potential traffic problems in getting there. Since we were both single, rather than going out, we made plans to grab a pizza and watch TV at his apartment.

This would be the second Valentine's Day that I'd spend without Sadie, the daughter I had raised since she was only eight months old. We had been together for nearly ten years, and we'd had an immensely close and loving bond.

When I awoke on Saturday morning, following my normal daily routine, I prayed. This time, however, I included a simple yet special prayer for Sadie. I asked God to throw so many coins on the ground near her throughout the day so that she would have absolutely no doubt that I was thinking of her. The reason this is significant is that, during my marriage, I bought God boxes for my wife, the two kids, and myself. We'd play a game finding pennies, nickels, dimes, and quarters on the ground—then save them in our boxes. Sadie had a blast ribbing me every time she found any coins.

Five minutes after asking God to fulfill that request for Sadie, I was set to begin driving to Rancho Mirage. I went outside to load my luggage into my car, which had been sitting idle for nine months. Upon opening the trunk, I immediately saw a rolled up reusable bag, which was puzzling because I didn't use those types of bags. Looking in it, I was shocked. There was approximately eight dollars in pennies, nickels, dimes, and quarters. I stood there perplexed as to how this could have happened. Almost instantaneously after I prayed to God about doing something for Sadie, it happened to me.

"But certainly, God has heard me;
He has attended to the voice of my prayer."
[NKJV Bible PSALM 66:19]

Still challenged by finding that mysterious bag of coins, minutes later I headed off in my car to buy a cup of coffee. At the cafe, I approached the counter and, surprisingly, there was a dime on the floor. I picked it up and put in my pocket.

Then I stopped at a convenience store to grab some snacks. While putting them onto the checkout counter, I saw another dime on the ground. So I snatched it up and dropped it into my pocket with the one that I had found minutes earlier. This was getting weird. With all the billions of people in the world, was God really listening to my prayers?

Stocked with coffee and some food to eat, I drove about an hour and a half before stopping in Phoenix to stretch my legs. Walking around a parking lot, I saw another dime and a penny on the ground. I plucked them up and added them to my morning's collection. Getting back into my car, my mind was racing as I thought about how seemingly improbable all of these "coincidences" were.

It was a beautiful, sunny day and—considering that it was the weekend—the traffic had been very light. That helped me to have a peaceful five-hour journey across the desert highway. Arriving at Everett's home in Rancho Mirage at approximately four in the afternoon, I was able to put my feet up and relax as he and I caught up on life—an opportunity that we both appreciated.

About six o'clock that evening, Everett decided to make a cocktail. While sipping it, he had an epiphany. He remembered that I was sober. As I could be his designated driver, Everett suggested that we head to Palm Springs and relish the nightlife there. We could watch TV at his place some other time.

Getting out at night was typically challenging for Everett because he owned a business in the area and worked long hours—seldom ever having the time or energy for a social life. With me at the wheel, though, Everett could relax and enjoy a rare evening of fun. Excited, we hopped into my car for the thirty-minute drive to Palm Springs, where I would experience the most incredible part of this story.

* * *

SADIE'S SONG

Arriving in Palm Springs, I immediately saw a lighted sign promoting a free outdoor concert featuring The Spinners, which began at seven o'clock. I mentioned to Everett how great our timing was, as it was only about ten minutes till seven. Looking to my right, I saw the concert stage in the outdoor lot of a local casino. My challenge now was where to park on such a busy night.

I pulled over in front of a fire hydrant to get my car off the street. Everett stated that I couldn't park there. I politely mentioned to him that I just wanted to look around the area to see if there might be an empty parking space. Everett then said emphatically that there was no possibility of that happening. It was time, however, to add to the list of the day's improbable occurrences.

Seconds later, the car directly in front of me pulled out of its parking space. It was right near the concert area. Jackpot! I drove forward and parked my car.

Now it was time to go and hear some great music from The Spinners, one of my favorite bands that I listened to growing up. Perhaps you may recall singing to some of their hits. They include "Games People Play," "The Rubberband Man," and "Working My Way Back to You."

Getting out of my car, Everett spotted the beer garden and we began walking there. Remarkably, he noticed a man wearing a t-shirt from the same small college that he had attended in Illinois, and began a conversation with him. Letting the two of them chat, I worked my way through the crowd and was able to find a place to stand about twenty feet from the concert stage. After being away for nearly a year, this was a great way to spend my first night back in California.

It was the middle of February, yet the temperature was warm, the sky was clear, and the moon was shining brightly—a perfect night to enjoy some musical memories. I stood there listening to and watching The Spinners, old and new. They looked spectacular in their all-white outfits. I was having a sensational time singing along to so many of their hit songs.

Nearly an hour after The Spinners began their performance, they said goodnight to the crowd and left the stage, but the concert was not over. Upon returning for an encore, The Spinners sang another one of their hits. Then they announced that their next number would be their last for the evening.

As The Spinners began performing the tune, I immediately got excited, but I was also puzzled. Although I recognized the music, I couldn't recall the name of the song. Then it hit me like a ton of bricks. I instantly grabbed my cellphone and started video recording The Spinners as they sang the song after which Sadie was named.

Early in our relationship, I asked my now ex-wife how she came to name Sadie. She told me that while driving in her mother's car one day, there was a Spinners CD playing. On it was a tune that really caught her attention—their 1974 hit called "Sadie." Feeling that it was such a beautiful ballad, my ex-wife decided that if she ever had a baby girl, she'd name her after that song.

While I stood there recording The Spinners, tears fell from my eyes. This truly couldn't be happening, but indeed it was—and right in front of me. Here I was witnessing the grand finale to one of the most improbable days of my life. The Spinners, with intense passion, repetitively sang: "Oh Sadie, sweet Sadie, how we love you sweet Sadie." It was almost as if they were actually singing to Sadie for me. They continued playing the song for more than seven minutes before saying good night.

Words cannot describe how I felt as The Spinners walked off the stage. I was nearly paralyzed with emotion thinking about the miraculous day that I'd just experienced.

There are tens of thousands of bands in the world and any one of them could have been on stage that night. Yet, there were The Spinners, singing the song "Sadie"—the exact song after which my ex-wife named my daughter. Unbelievably, it happened mere hours after I had prayed to God about her.

Now this is the confidence that we have in him,
that if we ask anything according to His will, He hears us.
And if we know that He hears us, whatever we ask,
we know that we have the petitions that we have asked of Him.
[NKJV Bible 1 John 5:14-15]

I am truly challenged trying to come up with the right words to describe how I feel as I think about this story and all of the perfectly aligned events that allowed it to happen. First, I had decided to leave Alaska and head to Arizona for a short vacation. Then I notified my aunt there of my plans. Her work schedule led me to adjust my itinerary. Thus, I flew to Arizona a few days later than I had originally scheduled. Otherwise, I would have already been back in Los Angeles on February 14, and this unlikely, but miraculous, story would've never happened.

Once in Arizona, I prayed to God, asking Him to shower Sadie with an enormous amount of coins on Valentine's Day. Moments later, I found a bag full of coins in the trunk of my car—a car which I hadn't used in nine months. Then I traveled three hundred and fifty miles to Rancho Mirage. At multiple locations along the way, I found and picked up more coins from the ground, keeping Sadie in my mind all day.

While at my friend Everett's, he had suggested that we abandon our original plan of watching TV and instead go out for the evening. So, we drove to Palm Springs on one of the busiest nights of the year and I was able to park in what seemed to be the best spot in town.

Finally, this improbable journey was capped off in an unimaginable fashion. The Spinners were appearing in concert on stage only a few feet in front of me. Unbeknownst to me at the time, they were accompanied by their last remaining original member, Henry Fambrough. He led The Spinners on stage as they sang the group's 1974 hit song, "Sadie." Amazingly, they performed it as their last number of the evening—wondrously positioned to where it had its greatest impact on me.

There's also another remarkable piece to this tale. As I was nearly done writing this chapter, I was on the internet researching information about The Spinners; what I found was fascinating.

Only two days before I filed for divorce, one of the two remaining original members of The Spinners, Bobby Smith, passed away. He along with his friend, Henry Fambrough, had performed together for more than fifty years. At that point, with his long-time partner gone, it would have seemed logical that Henry would simply retire. After all, he had enjoyed a career of which most musicians can only dream—but he never thought of bringing an end to The Spinners.

In stories that I read online, it was simply time for Henry to find a replacement for Mr. Smith and keep alive The Spinners' legacy. Had he not done so, again the nearly improbable ending to this saga would have never happened.

After witnessing all the events involved with this story, I can come to only one conclusion: when I was praying, *God was listening.*

CHAPTER 5: OUR LIVES FOREVER CHANGED

I married later in life, so I never figured that I would end up divorced. Nonetheless, as I shared in Chapter 3, life sometimes throws you curve balls and things change. My once happy marriage came to an end after nearly seven years.

Less than a week before filing for divorce, I moved out of my house and went to live with my best friend Johnny in his condo near Universal Studios Hollywood. A few days later, I submitted the paperwork to dissolve my marriage.

Shortly afterwards, I needed to bring some additional information to the court, which was about an hour-and-a-half commute one-way. I was grateful that Johnny agreed to ride along with me.

When we arrived at the courthouse, I spotted an empty parking space. Immediately upon pulling into it, the license plate on the car parked directly in front of us caught Johnny's eye. It read YURWILL. Sharing his discovery with me, Johnny said that it was obviously God's will that I was getting divorced.

Hearing that, I started thinking about many of the similar messages that I'd seen during the last year of my marriage. Johnny's comment appeared to be a true, albeit sad, statement. That license plate was just another in a vast series of such coincidental signs which had been continuously coming my way.

About a year before I separated from my wife, I co-signed a car loan for her to buy a Kia *Soul*. During our divorce process, it was repossessed. A week later, I stopped at a convenience store near Universal Studios Hollywood and, in the parking lot, was another Kia *Soul*. Its license plate was NHSGLRY, which I read as, *In His Glory*. Seeing that, I believed that God was telling me not to worry about my credit or anything else. He had everything under control.

"And we know that God causes everything to work together for the good of those who love God and are called according to His purpose for them."
[NLT Bible Romans 8:28]

A few months after my divorce was finalized, I saw another sign. Early one morning, I dropped my car off with my mechanic. That afternoon, when it was time to pick it up, I decided to hike the three miles to the repair shop. The sun was shining, and it was a beautiful California spring day. While enjoying my walk, I received a phone call from Kendra, a close friend of my sister.

During my marriage, Kendra had developed a kinship with my wife. I listened to Kendra as she told me that my now ex-wife had just called her and claimed that she had recently remarried. Right away I realized that that news came exactly one year after I filed for divorce.

Taking literally just three steps after hearing that news, I saw the words JESUS, GOD, and HOLY SPIRIT spray-painted on the sidewalk right in front of me. I stopped and stared in amazement at the timing of what I was seeing.

The coincidental signs that I've mentioned in this chapter, along with numerous others that I saw after separating from my wife, helped to confirm my belief that God had a meaningful purpose for me ending my marriage. What, though, could it possibly be?

While living at Johnny's condo, I broadcast my internet radio show, *In Your Face*, every Monday through Friday. The program focused on miracles and testimonies that had happened in the lives of my phone-in guests. Johnny listened to at least three shows per week from only a few feet away while sipping his coffee, even though—at that time—he wanted nothing to do with God. After every show, however, Johnny would say the same thing, "That was an interesting guest." Apparently, through the guests' testimonies, a seed of the Spirit of God was being planted in him.

After nearly a year of staying with Johnny, it was time to head off on my next adventure. I flew to Juneau for the jewelry sales job that I mentioned in Chapter 3. Although it was short-lived, I then ventured into the tourism business.

My first season in that industry wound up being tremendously rewarding, so I made arrangements to go back the following summer. Once the second season had ended in September, I decided to stay in Juneau through the month of October. I wanted to hang out with the black bears and to shoot more video for a reality TV concept that I had created.

* * *

A TRANSFORMING LIFE

One morning, during my extended Alaskan visit, Johnny sent me a text message asking if I could guess what he had bought. I responded that I had no idea. He replied that he purchased a Bible. Although excited for him, I was also puzzled. Johnny had a very nonspiritual upbringing and God was definitely not anyone that he desired in his life.

Having read those texts, I immediately called Johnny to find out why he had bought a Bible. He said that listening to the testimonies shared by guests on *In Your Face* got the ball rolling. Then Johnny mentioned that he met a woman who suggested that he might enjoy going to a service at Shepherd Church, which was not far from his home. Johnny claimed that he went there the following week and had a wonderful experience. Accordingly, he continued attending services there every Sunday for a month—even becoming a participant in the church's men's group.

Johnny shared all of this with me because he decided that he wanted to get baptized and turn his life over to Jesus. He hoped that I'd be there when it happened. I told Johnny that I could make it back to Los Angeles at the end of October. Therefore, he scheduled his ceremony for a Sunday in early November.

Three weeks after I talked with Johnny, I had secured the video that I needed for my reality TV concept and was finished visiting with the bears in Juneau. It was time for me to head to Los Angeles, where soon Johnny's life would be transformed.

Two days later, I was back in southern California, where I stayed with Johnny in his home. He spent the night excitedly talking about his upcoming life-changing event. It was as if he'd become a whole new person over the past several months. The following morning, he awoke and was so excited—like a little kid who had just found a favorite toy.

After sharing a very energetic and invigorating drive to Shepherd Church, Johnny and I entered the sanctuary, which held about fifteen hundred people. The crowd was filing in quickly, but we still managed to get a front-row seat. Johnny was all smiles as he told people around him about his big day. I sat next to him and enjoyed his newfound enthusiasm for life.

Twenty minutes later, the service began. Johnny and I joined in with the rest of the congregation and sang several songs, took communion, and listened to Pastor Dudley's sermon. Nearly an hour had passed and it was time for Johnny's life to be truly changed, transformed in a way that he had never experienced or anticipated.

Directly in front of us was a six-foot-high stage. On the left-hand side of it sat a small inflatable pool of water with a video camera focused on that area. A big-screen TV was in the middle of the stage to help the large congregation have a better viewpoint of what was about to take place. Pastor Dudley invited anyone in the large crowd who wanted to give his or her life to Jesus to come and stand next to the pool. Johnny got up, shook my hand, and made his way there. He stood all alone as the church band played some upbeat music. Gazing around the congregation, Johnny kept looking for someone to join him. Nearly every one of the seats in the sanctuary was filled, yet no one else walked up there.

A few minutes went by, the band stopped playing, and Johnny, resolute, continued to stand on stage alone. The moment had arrived. Pastor Martin took over the service and approached Johnny, and then both stepped into the pool. After introducing him to the audience, Pastor Martin asked Johnny two questions aimed at affirming his faith in Jesus. The instant Johnny said yes to the second question, he was dipped backwards into the water.

Soaked from head to toe, Johnny quickly stood up, pumping his arms above his head like he had just won a hard-fought boxing championship. Still in the pool, Johnny stared at his fellow church-goers. He was so excited. This middle-aged man, who had a very challenging upbringing, had found a new hope. There was now a new and almighty friend by his side—His name is Jesus.

Watching Johnny on stage showing off his undeniably new enthusiasm for life, I began a time of reflection. I started recalling the numerous coincidental signs that led me to leave my marriage and move into Johnny's condo. There he spent months listening to *In Your Face*—where, in so doing, he heard stories of miraculous transformations of people who, like him, had not believed in God. Notably, these life-altering experiences would not have happened for Johnny had I still been married.

Granted, those nearly seven years of marriage were a tremendously important part of my life. Raising two extremely loving and talented children with my wife was an incredible blessing. Thanks mainly to her efforts, my heart had been rekindled with a new and exciting fire for God, which led me to work on numerous projects for Him. I oversaw a church's homeless ministry, wrote my first spiritually themed book (*God Bless America...Before It's Too Late*), and started producing and hosting *In Your Face*.

During the time of my marriage, a wonderful passion for God was also ignited in my wife, our son Christopher, and our daughter Sadie. As I had done years earlier, all of them decided to get baptized and give their lives to Jesus. Then Anthony (Chapter 2) came into our lives and made the same decision. Now, Johnny had come to join the fold as well.

In the end, my marriage did not work out as *I* had planned. It did, however, appear to happen just as *God* had planned. For each one of us, these events led us to embrace our spirituality, and *all* of our lives had been forever changed.

CHAPTER 6: THE REALITY OF A HIGHER PURPOSE

So many times in my life, I believed that I knew the reason why I was striving toward a particular goal. However, as I'll show throughout this chapter, there apparently was a higher purpose for me chasing some of my dreams.

I previously stated that I worked in Alaska in the tourism industry. My first job was as a representative for a company that offered numerous excursions, including ziplining, dog-sledding, and walking on glaciers. Almost immediately after taking that position, my creative mind—honed from many years as a television producer—kicked in and gave me ideas I believed would make great reality TV shows.

Therefore, I began introducing myself to Juneau locals and business owners, sharing some details of my ideas with them. Right from the start, I received many positive responses. One entrepreneur told me that he had five boats, eight buses, and about thirty employees. He said that he'd make them all available to me if I needed them. Jackpot! I visited somewhere that I'd never been and, soon after, the prospect of producing my own network TV shows was looking like a sure reality.

The fact that I had several ideas would prove to be quite a challenge, though. I wouldn't have enough time to work at my job throughout the summer as well as capture video for each concept in order to create individual *sizzle* reels (i.e., video presentations used to sell concepts to a production company or network). Help would be much appreciated.

One afternoon in June, I was unexpectedly approached with a proposition by a new Alaskan friend, Bruce. He said that his son Hank worked at one of the major studios in Hollywood as a visual effects editor. Hank, though, wanted to pursue his dream of producing and directing, so he had purchased some professional video recording equipment. Bruce asked me if his son could shoot one of my reality TV concepts and said that Hank, at his own expense, would be willing to fly to Juneau. Another jackpot! Not only was I going to get some much-needed help, but direct from Hollywood. Plus it was free! Now, I needed to figure out with which of my ideas Hank could be the most helpful.

I had a project that I titled *The Real Deal*. It involved a brash businessman named Kevin who lived on a small Alaskan island about a twenty-minute flight from Juneau. Kevin was married, had three sons, and claimed that he was related to half of the approximately eight hundred residents on the island, many of whom were *Tlingits*— an indigenous clan of native Alaskans. In addition, Kevin said that he owned a whale-watching boat, was a bear guide, and operated a large-scale tree-trimming business. Kevin also mentioned that he had plenty of enemies in town. Bingo! From my perspective as a producer, having all of those dynamics to work with was exciting. This might be the perfect Alaskan reality TV show.

With all of that knowledge, and the possibility of capturing some awesome video, I felt that Hank would be a great partner for this project. I shared my decision with Bruce. He was excited for his son to have the opportunity to possibly advance his career. I was equally, if not more, elated to have Hank's knowledge and assistance.

Once I finalized plans to visit Kevin and his family on the small island, I told Hank and he bought a ticket to fly to Juneau. Soon I would have the opportunity to create one of my first sizzle reels. Accomplishing this goal was turning out to be a seemingly flawless process. Everything was falling into place perfectly, which made me feel that I was surely being guided by God.

Hank arrived in mid-July on a Friday afternoon. We were scheduled to shoot video with Kevin and his family during the next two days. Accordingly, on Saturday, Hank and I would be flying to meet them on our scheduled 8:00 a.m. flight. We'd be traveling in a small four-seat Cessna plane, so getting to the airport thirty minutes ahead of time was more than good enough. Unlike a regular commercial flight, there was no long security screening to go through. I planned to pick up Hank in the morning at seven o'clock at his hotel which was only ten minutes from Juneau airport.

A fairly thick fog filled the sky on Saturday morning, and I hoped it would not affect the flight that Hank and I were set to take. Nevertheless, I arrived as scheduled in downtown Juneau at Hank's hotel and met him in person for the first time. He seemed a bit shy but pleasant. Surprisingly, Bruce was also there. He had already bought his own ticket for our flight having decided to join us as Hank's assistant. I certainly had no problem with extra free help.

While Hank was loading his video equipment into my car, however, he and Bruce became irritated with each other. After a few minutes of bickering, Bruce decided that he would forego joining us. Without saying a word, he simply turned and walked away. Puzzled by his actions, I started my car and Hank and I headed to the airport.

Although short, our ten-minute ride there was uneasy for me. Hank was clearly stressed by the incident with his father. This worried me, as the last thing that I needed was Hank venting his frustrations to Kevin and his family, especially because I hadn't yet met any of them. They were expecting to meet professional Hollywood TV producers. Anything less might bring a sudden end to this show concept.

Once I parked my car at the airport, Hank and I walked inside the terminal, where our pilot escorted us to the small Cessna plane that would take us on our brief flight to meet Kevin. The distance was only about eighty miles. Saying that he had flown this route many times before, our pilot told us that the fog would not have an effect on our flight. With Hank and me as the only two passengers, we took off as scheduled.

Nearly twenty minutes later, at about eight thirty, the plane landed on the small island. Kevin met us on the tarmac as we exited the Cessna. Our host was wearing overalls, a t-shirt, and a baseball cap. Standing about six feet tall, Kevin was built like a grizzly bear and had a giant personality to match. Even more remarkable was that our flight over the beautiful Alaskan landscape appeared to relax Hank. He was now much more tranquil, which definitely gave me a sense of comfort. After sharing some pleasantries with Kevin, we were off to meet his family.

Arriving at Kevin's simple, single-family home, he introduced Hank and me to his wife and three sons, along with a few friends. Then Kevin showed us the guest house where we would stay later that night. Before we'd get any sleep though, there was a full day ahead with plenty of video to capture. Kevin's plans for us included reeling in the halibut lines that he had dropped a day earlier. We would also pull up some crab pots, search for brown bears, and watch a native tribal dance.

Our day's activities began with a trip down to the docks to see Kevin's fishing boat. Two of his sons and one of their friends, along with Hank and myself rode there with Kevin in his van. Kevin's father, who we called Grandpa, also met us there. Hank caught video of their playful conversations and some great male bonding as they hung out on the docks. Grandpa led the banter, along with Kevin and his boys. I listened, laughed, and learned about their lives and relationships, which would be a major part of *The Real Deal*.

Next, all of us but Grandpa headed out on Kevin's well-worn boat. We spent a few hours cruising the Alaskan waters as he and his sons reeled in nearly six hundred and fifty pounds of halibut from lines they laid out the day before. All the while, Hank recorded video of them.

* * *

FROM MISERY TO BLESSING

Throughout this trip, Kevin and his sons kept asking Hank about his father, Bruce, although none of them had ever met him. They also were not aware of the situation earlier that morning in Juneau when Bruce walked away from us. Somewhat irritated by their questioning, Hank's apparent frustration grew as the guys pursued answers. Surely, this wasn't how he figured this weekend would unfold.

Heading back to the docks from the day's fishing adventure, Kevin stopped his boat in a small cove where, a few days earlier, he had placed some crab pots in the water. One of his sons pulled up three of them onto our boat and each pot contained several Dungeness crabs. I was excited to see them as this allowed Hank to capture some nice video.

Next, Kevin drove us to the home of one of his native *Tlingit* relatives, where we dropped off some of the freshly caught halibut. We brought the rest of the fish and the crabs to Kevin's house. His wife would eventually cook some of the day's catch for our dinner. With plenty of work still left for us to do, however, that wouldn't be for a while.

At about three o'clock in the afternoon, Hank and I hopped into Kevin's truck with him and went to visit some of his arch rivals. I learned quickly that Kevin's adversaries truly disliked him—partly because of his aggressive personality, and also for being a successful businessman on a mostly poor, native island. Hank captured video of some spirited conversations between Kevin and a few of his foes. Those heated interactions would be a great addition to my sizzle reel for *The Real Deal.*

Now nearly four-thirty in the afternoon, it was time to find some brown bears. Driving around the back roads of the island, Kevin continued to question Hank about his relationship with Bruce. One comment after another, Kevin continually bombarded Hank about the importance of a good father-and-son relationship. From the look on Hank's face, he was obviously very uncomfortable listening to Kevin. Making matters worse was the reality that Hank couldn't just walk away. Kevin was driving us around on an unfamiliar—and possibly dangerous—island that Hank had never visited. Thus, hopping out of the truck and walking home simply was not an option.

Throughout this bear search, we certainly saw plenty of evidence that they existed. Unfortunately, we did not see any actual bears. After three hours of looking for them, I was hungry and tired, so I thanked Kevin for his efforts and suggested that it was time to eat dinner. Hank could not have been happier!

Even so, there was one more stop that we first needed to make. Kevin had arranged for a group of *Tlingits* to perform for us. We headed back into town where we met twelve Tribe members, including the Tribal leader and his assistant. They warmly and humbly greeted us, wearing colorful native garments, while Hank captured them on video. We learned that each member's clothing

Rob Ekno

(including robe and headdress) was designed uniquely for each individual based on their name, family, and personality traits.

The two adult leaders led a group of mostly teenage members who sang and chanted two lively songs while dancing traditional *Tlingit* movements which portrayed important stories and aspects of their culture. It was such an incredible experience to witness. Their gift to us lasted about twenty minutes; we then expressed our gratitude, thanking each member individually. I was deeply moved and felt greatly honored that they went out of their way to share this intimate portrait of themselves with us.

After saying our good-byes, we headed to Kevin's house. When we arrived there, the living room was full of family and friends who stopped by to meet Hank and me. As everyone told stories and shared a few laughs, Hank kept his camera rolling. The camaraderie exhibited by this group of people would surely be another important aspect of *The Real Deal*.

Finally, it was time for dinner. Kevin's father-in-law led the meal with a prayer. We had Dungeness crab and fresh halibut pizza, a specialty of Kevin's wife. It was really good! Afterwards, Hank and I interviewed some of Kevin's family and a few of their guests. Then it was time for the two of us to get a good night's sleep.

The next morning, Sunday, I needed to fly back to Juneau. Hank stayed on the island to get some video of Kevin and his family at church. Consequently, this left Kevin more time to continue his conversations with Hank about father-son relationships. I have no idea what transpired after I left the two of them. Apparently, though, it was something truly miraculous!

About eight-thirty that Sunday night, I received a call from Bruce, who told me that he could not thank me enough for what I'd done to Hank on our trip. I had no idea what he was talking about. Continuing on, Bruce explained that his relationship with Hank had been extremely strained for the past ten years. Although Bruce wanted to help Hank with this project, after their emotional conversation at my car on Saturday morning, he felt that it was best not to come with us.

As our call progressed, Bruce said that he went to pick up Hank at the Juneau airport a few minutes earlier when he had returned from the island. Bruce claimed that Hank exited the baggage area, then unexpectedly put his camera equipment onto the sidewalk and rushed over to hug him. Hank told Bruce that he was truly sorry for being such a challenging son, and that he wanted to make things right between the two of them. Incredible! The result of that weekend's experience was completely unpredictable, yet amazing!

At the time that I finished writing this story, neither my dream of selling *The Real Deal* nor Hank's dream of becoming a producer or director had been realized. However, in Hollywood terms, our weekend on that island could be referred to as a real award-winning, red-carpet event. Thanks to Kevin and his sons, Hank was able to realize the importance of the father-son relationship—which also proved to be a major blessing for his dad, Bruce.

So, in the end, it wasn't *The Real Deal* that took home top honors from our weekend of chasing dreams. Rather, the *Oscar* went to the more improbable story, *The Reuniting of a Father and Son.*

I had created several reality TV show concepts. Hank could have been of help to me on any one of them. Interestingly, for some reason, I chose that one.

A man's heart plans his way,
but the Lord directs his steps.
[NKJV Bible Proverbs 16:9]

---

* * *

BROTHERS IN ARMS

This is the story of another TV show idea that I conceived. It centered around two best friends in Juneau, Jake and Hunter, who owned and operated the most unique and exotic indoor shooting range and gun store in Alaska. These two guys both had larger-than-life personalities that fit their towering physical presence. Both were rugged outdoorsmen: Jake was husky, clean-cut, and mild mannered, while Hunter was of slighter build, sported a bushy goatee, and was blunt and outspoken—having no problem telling you what he thought of you.

Being survivalists at heart, Jake's and Hunter's gun enterprise was born out of their staunch determination to protect their families in case the world was soon coming to an end. They got into this business after having amassed a collection of hundreds of guns and thousands of rounds of ammunition over several years. The two buddies stored this gigantic stockpile inside a large metal storage container tucked inside a hole they dug in a small mountain in Jake's back yard. The site was mostly obscured by some construction vehicles they owned for another business they shared, but they were still able to access the firearm collection as needed. Somehow, the guys kept all of this hidden from their wives for several years but, unfortunately for the men, the ladies eventually discovered the massive cache of weapons.

Once the dust settled after their initial shock, the wives insisted that their husbands get rid of their prized collection. Rather than selling them all, however, Jake and Hunter looked for investors to build out the dream gun store facility that they had conjured up from an idea they picked up in Vegas. Thus, the two buddies would be able to keep their own guns, but would also sell new inventory they would buy.

Through lots of hard work and determination, Jake and Hunter were able to raise nearly three million dollars. That allowed them to craft one of the nicest gun stores and shooting ranges in America. In addition to housing the guns there, their main goal was to get rich from the newfound "Tourism Gold Rush" in Alaska. Cruise ship passengers could now shoot a variety of firearms—including historic and automatic weapons in the friends' state-of-the-art facility. Additionally, classes and training were offered for people who wanted to learn proper gun use and safety.

As a producer, I saw numerous dynamics and storylines in and out of the gun range around which to build an exciting reality TV show. They included the relationship between Jake and Hunter and their families. Also, quite often people came into the store looking to sell rare and intriguing firearms collections. That led to some energetic and sometimes heated bargaining sessions. For those reasons and more, I approached the two partners with my idea titled *Brothers in Arms*. (It was sort of a mash-up of *Diners, Drive-ins and Dives* meets *Pawn Stars* in *Alaska: The Last Frontier*.) They loved it!

In addition to liking my show concept, Jake and Hunter offered me a job as their tour sales manager, which I accepted. From a small booth on the cruise ship docks, I would be selling vouchers allowing people to shoot celebrated firearms, including a Gatling gun, a Thompson submachine gun, and several others.

Along with marketing the tours, I also needed to capture enough video for an exciting sizzle reel to sell *Brothers in Arms*. That proved to be quite trying as I spent lots of energy and long hours pitching the gun packages six days a week. Even more bothersome was that, at the end of each shift, I'd visit the shooting range, where employees would tell me great stories from their day—stories that would make very compelling TV. I was excited to hear them, but also extremely frustrated because I wasn't able to record any of those great moments. It was just another obstacle that I would have to overcome while pursuing my dream.

I spent five months selling tours from the docks before the grind of the summer season came to an end. Sales were dismal and not nearly as lucrative as we had hoped. There was one major reason: unlike the helicopter and whale-watching excursions, the well-known cruise ship lines would not promote our *gun* tours for fear of liability.

More discouraging was the fact that I wasn't able to acquire much video to help me sell *Brothers in Arms*. Therefore, I told Jake and Hunter that I planned to stay in Juneau for another month and continue working on this show. Daily, I would hang out at their store and hopefully get what I needed.

My first day there, however, I was blindsided. Hunter told me that he had decided to take a three-week vacation with his wife, Sharon, and they would be leaving Juneau the very next day. *Say what?*

Here I was sacrificing my time and energy to create a reality TV show around their business, and I was mystified as to why Jake and Hunter didn't seem as committed as me to this project. Yes, selling this show would obviously help my career, but airing on national TV would catapult their business as well. Yet two of the four main characters didn't even see fit to tell me that they would be leaving town. Undoubtedly, I'd be able to record some of the store employees and customers while they were gone, but I would still need video of Hunter and Sharon. Since they wouldn't be returning to work until the day before I left Juneau, I'd need a lot more than my fingers crossed to be able to create a great sizzle reel.

During the next few weeks, I did manage to capture some nice pieces of video. Through my eyes as a producer, I was excited to watch a range of interactions among the gun store's employees, which were most often playful, but could sometimes be quite intense. One day I walked in on an unusually heated conversation between

Jake and the business manager regarding that summer's lack of sales. Not long after, the business manager left the company.

Several patrons also provided me the opportunity to get some great video. (For instance, one man walked in with a hand grenade that his father had on his fireplace mantle for decades! A quick inspection and search of the serial number by a store employee determined that it was indeed a live grenade. It was swiftly shuttled outside without incident.)

Finally, the day before I was leaving Juneau, Hunter and Sharon returned to work at the gun store. Plenty of energetic people visited them, and I was able to grab some good footage of their interactions. A gentleman also stopped by looking to sell an exotic collection of firearms, which led to some serious negotiations before he sold them. It took a while, but I ultimately got the video that I wanted to help me sell *Brothers in Arms.*

There was only one thing left for me to do—something that I should have done months before: get Jake or Hunter to sign a working agreement allowing me to sell the show. When I presented the paperwork to Hunter, though, I received an unexpected hard time from him. He was unwilling to sign the typical twelve-month deal that I needed in order to shop *Brothers in Arms* around Hollywood.

Having worked with Hunter all summer, his uncooperative response caught me completely off guard. He explained to me that he truly loved my *Brothers in Arms* idea—so much so that, for several weeks, he had been having conversations about the show. The problem was, those discussions were not with *me.* Instead, Hunter had been talking with a big-time Hollywood production company. They already had a successful Alaskan-based reality TV show on a major network. Talk about getting whacked from behind!

For months I worked on *Brothers in Arms* on my own time and expense. Now I get told this heart-breaking news from Hunter. Wow, that was another BIG lesson that I learned as I pursued my dream.

73

Knowing that I could not move forward on the show without an agreement, I needed another plan. My brain promptly went into overdrive. About thirty minutes later, I came up with an idea.

I convinced Hunter to sign a three-month contract with a stipulation that could eventually get me what I needed. The caveat was that I had to get another entity to work with me on *Brothers in Arms*. That could be an experienced reality TV producer, a production company, or a network. If I accomplished that during our three-month agreement, it would automatically convert to twelve months. At last, I had plenty of video and a contract in my hand. It was now time to find a partner and put together the presentation package necessary to sell *Brothers in Arms*. Hollywood here I come!

Having no one immediately lined up to help me, I began my search right away. Walking out of the gun store, I phoned my friend Walter in Los Angeles and explained my situation to him. He told me that he'd contact his friend Steve, who was a veteran reality TV producer.

The next day, Walter called and said that Steve wanted me to email him my concept for *Brothers in Arms*. I did so a few minutes later before flying out of Juneau. Hopefully, Steve would become my producing partner.

In any event, before I could go back to Hollywood, I needed to visit some family members in Arizona. Eight hours after leaving Juneau, I arrived there thinking about my recent challenges in dealing with *Brothers in Arms*. I was truly puzzled by the headaches that I had experienced the other day in dealing with the agreement. Perhaps it was time for me to focus on another one of my show ideas.

At five o'clock the next morning, however, I was on my knees praying. I asked God if He wanted me to continue putting together the presentation reel for *Brothers in Arms*. At the exact same time that I asked Him that question, in another room, I heard the bell on my cellphone, indicating that I had a text message. Once finished with my prayers, I went to see who was contacting me so early. Grabbing my phone, I noticed that the text was from my friend, Pastor Larry, in Indiana. I had only met him once in my life a few years earlier.

His text read:

> *Rob there has been a very systematic and complex attack set upon you. I am supposed to tell you not to give up on yourself, not to give up on your ideas and not to give up on the people who are giving you all the crap. Within this group, which have become more enemies than partners, is your Jonathan, and he will rise up to stand with you and help you finish your heart's desire. Your creative genius is actually the mind of Christ working in you and it is being resisted by principalities and powers. Take this fight back to the spirit realm and use the weapons that are not carnal but mighty to the pulling down of strongholds. I have got your back here in intercession. God wants these projects in your heart done and completed. Get up, you're a warrior.*

Incredible! I asked God what I was supposed to do regarding *Brothers in Arms* and I received my answer instantaneously, perhaps in the most inexplicable way imaginable.

I recalled the story from the Old Testament where Jonathan helped to keep his father, King Saul, from harming David. Who exactly among the owners and their partners was *my* Jonathan? I'm not exactly sure.

After making a cup of coffee, I called Pastor Larry—who had no idea that I was working on this project—to discuss his text. He stated that he had been praying earlier that morning and God made it very clear to him that he needed to deliver that message to me. As I have learned, sometimes God answers quickly, sometimes slowly. That morning it was instantly. Like He knew what I was going to pray for before I even woke up. God then gave the answer to a man that He knew would deliver it to me. More importantly, God gave the answer to a man whom He knew that I would trust.

A few days later, Steve and I signed a deal to work together on *Brothers in Arms.* Now, my original three-month agreement with Jake and Hunter was extended to twelve months—just what I wanted. As soon as the ink on the contract with Steve had dried, we called the two buddies and told them of our partnership. After they interrogated Steve for twenty minutes, they felt good about our chances of selling the show.

I spent the next several weeks sorting through and editing numerous hours of video. Eventually, I put together an exciting sizzle reel for us to shop around Hollywood.

Three days later, I received a call from Steve. He said that he had been invited to New York to meet with a major TV network. Executives there wanted to discuss the possibility of him working on one of their shows. Steve then told me that during his meeting with them he would share *Brothers in Arms.* Jackpot! This was a huge break for me—quite possibly the one that I needed to sell my show.

However, later that day, everything changed in a flash. As Steve was flying to his meeting in New York, at the same time, in Dallas, a tragic event involving guns occurred. Five people were killed in a shooting spree, and the shocking story made national headlines. Upon landing, Steve received several calls from friends in Hollywood telling him not to share my idea with the network right now, but rather to save it for a later date. It would seem that the timing for our show about guns was now less than favorable to say the least. Instead, it was time to keep a respectful silence and let the country mourn.

This situation taught me another lesson. You can work hard and do all the seemingly right things to fulfill your dreams. However, sometimes setting your dreams aside, in this case to let people heal, is the right thing to do.

I began thinking about the text that I got from Pastor Larry. Had I not received it, most likely I would have decided to forego any more work on this show concept and move on to another one. Yet, once I reread that message, I felt strongly that God wanted me to eventually regroup and continue onward with *Brothers in Arms*.

After several months had passed, friends in Hollywood began telling me that the climate had changed and that I should once again try to sell the show. Listening to their advice, I contacted Jake and Hunter to let them know of my plan. They were excited to get my call; however, before I could move forward, I would have to get video of their new employees to update the sizzle reel. There was still time left on our twelve-month agreement, so I would not immediately need to deal with the possible headache of them signing a new one.

When our conversation ended, I swiftly moved into action planning my next visit to Juneau. Steve wouldn't be joining me on this trip as he had become involved in another TV project—although he'd still help me to sell *Brothers in Arms* once I created a new sizzle reel.

* * *

YOU HAD US FROM HELLO

In search for additional footage for the reel, I arrived in downtown Juneau in early April at the apartment of my friend, Samuel. Only a block away was the city's homeless facility. Unlike its neatly kept, grey-faced building, there were a lot of unkempt individuals who went there daily to receive a meal, take a shower, or have a bed for the evening.

Except for the time that these folks were using the homeless facility, they spent a good portion of their days hanging out in groups nearby talking with each other, and regularly entertaining themselves with unhealthy activities. These included sharing a can of beer, shooting heroin, or planning their next shoplifting excursion.

As previously mentioned, I was homeless for a time back when, and I can certainly relate to the plight of a lot of these people. I suffered much of the same with addiction, etc., that they were facing...and my heart feels for them. Still, I'm also well aware of the emotional and personality challenges many homeless people have, and so I'm always on my guard when I pass by them—never knowing if a word or mere eye contact will set someone off.

On this trip to Juneau, every morning I'd hike past the homeless facility on my way to a twelve-step meeting I regularly attended about a half a mile away. The first couple of days, I felt uneasy and a bit intimidated when walking by the various groups that would always be assembled along my route. I didn't know any of these people, nor their histories, so I would do as most do and simply stroll by, hoping there would be no interruption or incident. I'd keep an eye open behind me as I passed by them, just to make sure no one was coming up to harm me. When I strode by these folks, I was somewhat fearful, and wouldn't begin to relax until about a block after I passed them.

Personally, I would hate to have this same experience happen in my head every day. I constantly wondered if I'd be robbed, stabbed, or worse?

For some reason, after about a week of these stressful walks, I made my way by a group of homeless men, and found myself blurting, "Hey, guys, how are you? You're not going to hit me today are you?" Where I came up with that I had no idea, but it worked. I could see a couple of them smile, which gave me some peace...so I continued to use that phrase every time I saw a similar gathering over the next couple of weeks. Each time I did so, I received the same response—until one day.

IS IT GOD OR COINCIDENCE?

I was heading home from a morning meeting when I passed by eight men huddled in a circle. Feeling much more comfortable in their presence, in my usual fashion, I said, "Hey, guys, how are you? You're not going to hit me today are you?" Surprisingly, one of the men responded, "No, dude, we'd *never* hit you." I was caught off guard by his remark but immediately (and politely) replied, "Thank you, I appreciate that," and continued walking.

However, after a few steps, something told me to stop. I needed to go back and ask the guy why he'd said that to me. Turning around, I ambled up to the group and questioned the man about that comment. His explanation stunned me.

The man said that he and his friends hung out in downtown Juneau every day with *at least a couple of hundred people* passing by them. He stated, "You're the only person who ever says 'hi' to us, so you'd be the *last* person that we'd hit." The guy told me, "Our lives are a mess right now, but because you say 'hi' to us, we feel that someone cares about our well-being, and it gives us hope that someday we might be able to turn our lives around."

As I recall, I thanked the gentleman for his comments, and wished him and his friends a good day. Then, as I turned to continue down the street, tears began to flow from my eyes. Instead of going home, I decided to go to the docks to sit there and process what I just experienced.

Wow.... Talk about an eye-opener!

"Kind words can be short and easy to speak,
but their echoes are truly endless."
Mother Teresa

There was another blessing to come out of my encounter with those homeless men in Juneau, which I experienced a few days later when I returned to Los Angeles. During a twelve-step meeting in a church there, I shared the tale of me saying "hi" to that group. Two weeks later in the same building, I went to a similar gathering. The leader for the day failed to show up and I was asked to fill in for him. Looking around the room, I counted about seventy-five people. Seeing many faces that I didn't recognize, I decided to again tell that same story.

After reiterating my experience, a woman named Lisa, sitting in the back of the meeting, began speaking. Mentioning she'd been there when I originally told that story, Lisa stated that I shamed her. I had no idea what she was talking about. Lisa then said that every weekday for the past couple of years, she had been walking by the same homeless woman. Never once had she ever said "hi" to her. Hearing of my involvement with the group in Juneau impacted Lisa hard. Now compelled to act differently, for the last two weeks, she had been having daily conversations with that lady. Here was another reminder that one never knows what may materialize through a small act of kindness.

* * *

HE HANDED ME THE KNIFE

Back in Juneau, at a twelve-step meeting a few days before my encounter with that homeless group, I met a rugged, athletic-looking, thirty-something newcomer named Ben. We had a brief conversation about his struggle to stop drinking and using drugs. I offered him my phone number should he ever want help staying sober. We then hugged and went our separate ways.

Nearly two weeks had gone by since that meeting and I had not again seen Ben until one afternoon. Walking in downtown Juneau, I spotted him in the middle of the street coming my way, barely able to stand up, apparently impaired by alcohol, drugs, or both. There were two other guys and a woman walking with Ben. Nevertheless, I decided to hop into the street, void of any oncoming cars, and calmly ask him why he was stumbling along. He could hardly get a word out in response.

Fearing for Ben, I got "in his face" and began telling him that God had a better plan for his life than the way he was living. My rebuke lasted only about a minute; however, I could see the fearful look in his friends' eyes signaled that Ben was about ready to clobber me. From our prior conversation, I knew that he had grown up in a very challenging neighborhood. So, it was likely that Ben had seen a fight or two along the way. Knowing that he was an alcoholic justified my thought process. Hopefully, I hadn't gone too far in confronting him.

Shockingly, instead of hitting me, Ben started crying and stepped my way, wrapped his arms tightly around my shoulders, and thanked me. As he stepped back, Ben caught me completely off guard. He pulled his right jacket sleeve up to his elbow revealing three long slices in his forearm that went from his wrist to his elbow. Sadly, a short time before I saw him that day, Ben had used a knife trying to kill himself. Seeing this, I was now really jacked up and went at him even stronger with God talk.

Ben's friends looked at me like I had finally gone overboard. The look in their eyes told me that he was definitely going to pound me into the ground. However, I've found that it's tough to argue with God. So, rather than punch me, Ben calmly reached into his jacket and pulled out a medium-sized pocket knife, and handed me the blood-spattered weapon. He then hugged me again, thanked me for talking to him, and put his arm around his woman friend. Slowly, they turned away from me and continued their trek down the street. Incredible! This could not be happening, but indeed it was.

I stood there looking at Ben's dried blood on that knife. The feeling of how blessed I was to be sober filled my soul. Watching Ben walk off into an unknown future, though, broke my heart. Especially since I knew that if he truly wanted help, it was waiting for him—and it was free.

Over the past couple of years, I have contacted some of Ben's acquaintances in Juneau to inquire about his well-being. They reportedly still see him around the city on a regular basis, which has often led me to wonder whether those two encounters with Ben were mere coincidences? Or were they, in fact, miraculous acts of God?

$$* * *$$

I NEED TO TALK...NOW!

The night after my encounter with Ben, I was approached by a man named Lance, whom I had also previously met at a recovery meeting in Juneau. Lance was homeless, in his late-twenties, and he appeared jittery and somewhat unkempt. I was taping some video on the cruise ship docks when he came and sat on one of the log pilings a few feet behind my camera and tripod. As I finished a segment, Lance waved and said "hi." I responded politely and continued to record my next bit. This time when I stopped, he asked me if we could talk. I told Lance that I was really tired, and that I needed to quickly finish shooting my project as the sun was setting fast. He didn't respond, but continued to sit and watch me.

When I was done with my work, Lance stood up and was emphatic that we talk now. I had given him my phone number at our previous meeting and told him to call me if I could ever be of any assistance in his efforts to stay sober. (He'd been struggling for fifteen years.)

Even so, I reiterated how dead tired I was and asked if we could chat the next day. Lance was unphased and firmly insisted that we have our conversation immediately. Ordinarily I'd bend over backward for any newcomer who needs help, but I was barely able to stand up from exhaustion, and didn't think that I could be any value to him at that moment.

It was now eight in the evening, and God gave me a little nudge, reminding me of my morning prayers. I had asked Him to show me how I could be of maximum service to Him and my fellows throughout the day. God alerted me to the fact that it was still *today* and that I didn't put a time restriction on my request.

Prompted by my *Higher Power*, I knew that I had to talk with Lance now, so I told him that I'd go and speedily freshen up, then treat him to a pizza. Displaying a sense of calmness after hearing my plan, Lance patiently waited for me at the bottom of the stairs outside of my apartment.

The sun had set and the temperature had dropped considerably. Having put on warmer clothing, I walked down to meet Lance, then led him a couple of blocks over to the pizzeria as we were both starving. I placed an order to go, anticipating that what he wanted to share with me needed some privacy.

Taking the pizza, we made our way over to the cruise ship docks and Marine Park—a popular nighttime hangout for the local homeless population. Fortunately, they had not already gathered there. I figured that Lance and I would take advantage of this rare time of quiet in the park.

Sitting on the edge of a large, three-foot-high concrete structure, we ate our pizza as Lance began detailing intimate stories about his life, including his long battle for sobriety. Chief among Lance's challenges was in not being able to see his young daughter back in California because his ex didn't want him around, and of how much suffering this brought him on a daily basis. The frustration of not being sober was agonizing to Lance, and had become completely overwhelming. Those are just two of a litany of pains and struggles that he lived with and he was now at a breaking point.

Having been sober for more than two decades at the time, hearing such stories was not unique to me. Yet, it was unusual for Lance to voice them, since he had never told these things to *anyone*. Why he chose to divulge his struggles to me rather than someone he knew better, I don't know. Maybe the fact that I was an outsider, not a Juneau resident, made it easier for Lance to confide in me. All I know is that it seemed that the more that Lance spoke, the more relief and peace he felt. That's all that mattered.

Nearly an hour and a half after beginning to bare his soul to me, Lance still had plenty left in him that he wanted to discuss. Admittedly, I was completely exhausted—it was about ten at night and groups of homeless people had now found their way around us.

Knowing that this conversation was important to Lance, I suggested that we find somewhere else with more privacy. So we crossed the street and began climbing a set of metal stairs heading toward Mount Roberts. Halfway up the 110-step staircase, we came upon an old wooden platform that overlooked the cruise ship docks. No one else was there, so Lance and I decided to stay and continue our dialogue.

The cool wind blew gently and the moon shined down upon us. Lance spent the next two and a half hours revealing to me some truly excruciating trials and situations that he had lived with throughout his life.

In all, Lance spent four hours that night sharing from deep down in his heart and soul, telling me, a nearly complete stranger, things that he probably would have taken to the grave. We were now both quite cold, along with being physically and emotionally drained. Thankfully, I could clearly see the relief in Lance's face and his relaxed state of being. I was certainly glad that God had moved me to meet with him that night.

As we were set to leave, Lance told me that he really appreciated me listening to him and that he loved me. Wow! I gave him a hug then we walked down the long staircase to the street and went our separate ways.

Talk about an adventurous and rewarding month in Juneau! I was simply looking to capture video to create a sizzle reel for a TV show concept. God evidently had other plans for my being there.

"For I know the plans I have for you, declares the LORD,
plans to prosper you and not to harm you,
plans to give you hope and a future."
[NLT Bible Jeremiah 29:11]

In the end, my goal for going back to Juneau was accomplished. I secured the video that I needed to help me sell *Brothers in Arms*. However, as I previously mentioned, the show has not yet sold. There are some very good reasons why.

A few weeks after returning to Los Angeles, I called Jake and Hunter at the gun store to let them know that Steve would be showing our new presentation reel to some friends in Hollywood. Once again, I was caught off guard by what I was told. Those two best friends of nearly twenty years had ended their business relationship. Hunter had moved to another state with his wife and kids. Welcome to Hollywood.

Seriously, I worked on that project for nearly a year and a half. I spent hundreds of hours capturing and editing video. On my own dime, I flew back and forth multiple times between Los Angeles and Juneau. Now I was blindsided again, being told that two of the four main characters in the show were gone.

I could have still tried to sell this concept, but I would have had to start from scratch with several new gun store employees. Also, two more tragic incidents involving firearms had taken place which made national headlines—a school shooting in Florida, and another shooting spree at a concert in Las Vegas.

Consequently, I examined the situations that occurred while pursuing my dream to create reality TV shows. I am now completely convinced that I have truly fulfilled the real mission that God had for me in pursuing both *The Real Deal* and *Brothers in Arms.* Clearly, He used my efforts and determination to achieve my dream for a higher purpose than my own.

Furthermore, as I was in the final stages of writing this chapter, I decided to call my friend Anthony in Anacortes, Washington. During our conversation, I shared the stories in this chapter with him. Anthony told me that my experiences reminded him of his favorite quote from Mother Teresa:

> *"God doesn't require us to succeed,*
> *He requires that you try."*

Amen.

CHAPTER 7: IT'S A WONDERFUL LIFE

The movie *It's a Wonderful Life* is one of the most classic and beloved films of all time. You would think that as a baby boomer I had seen the picture at least once by the time I was fifty, but no, that was not the case. Even more, I had absolutely no idea what the movie was about. Fortunately, my friend Walter invited me to the 70th anniversary screening of the film, which took place one cool December evening in Beverly Hills.

To get to the event, Walter and I decided to make the twenty-minute drive in his car. We met at a convenient location in Studio City that was directly over the Hollywood Hills from Beverly Hills. Our destination on Wilshire Boulevard was the Samuel L. Goldwyn Theatre, which belongs to the Academy of Motion Picture Arts and Sciences.

There was event parking in an underground garage across the street from the theatre. We arrived only a few minutes before the opening of the pre-screening festivities. The line of cars in front of us was long as there were many impatient drivers looking for parking spaces. Free *hors d'oeuvres* and beverages were awaiting them in the theatre lobby.

While Walter and I calmly waited for an available spot, I saw something perplexing. A gentleman driving a minivan was trying to fit into a compact space. Clearly, it was impossible for the driver to get into that opening—not without damaging the small hatchback to its right. A few seconds later, I heard the sound of metal on metal. Sure enough, the minivan scraped against the right rear quarter panel of the hatchback.

Curiously, the motorist backed the vehicle out of that space without ever looking at the car that he hit. Instead, the guy proceeded to drive behind a concrete wall in another section of the parking garage. My instincts told me to hop out of Walter's sedan and follow him. I wanted to make sure that he was going to come back and leave a note on the car that he damaged.

Walking around the wall, I was then standing about fifteen feet behind the (now parked) minivan. The middle-aged male driver got out and casually walked to the passenger's side, which had several scrapes from his brush against the hatchback. Using his shirt sleeve, the man tried to rub out any evidence of damage to his vehicle. All the while, he had no idea that I was watching him, nor did he have any clue that I witnessed the accident.

The guy continued his polishing efforts for several minutes, but was not able to buff out all of the damage to his minivan. Then he opened its passenger side door and grabbed a new shirt from the back seat. He took off the one that he was wearing and threw it in his vehicle. Thereupon the man put on the new shirt and locked the minivan. Seemingly, without a care, he nonchalantly walked up the exit ramp of the underground parking structure.

Witnessing that, I concluded that the driver had no intention of leaving a note on the damaged hatchback. So, I pulled out my cellphone and took pictures of his license plate and the scrapes on his vehicle, then I walked back to find Walter. He had now parked and was a bit anxious about us getting into the theatre.

First, though, I shared with him what I witnessed. Next, I wrote a note on my business card stating that I had seen the entire incident, and then placed the card on the driver's side window of the damaged car.

He has shown you, O man, what is good;
And what does the Lord require of you
But to do justly.
[NKJV Bible Micah 6:8]

Walter and I now made our way out of the parking structure and into the pre-screening festivities. The theatre lobby was filled with pictures and memorabilia from the movie. We each took numerous photographs of the various displays, and enjoyed some complementary food and drinks.

I went into the theatre with Walter following closely behind after about thirty minutes of carousing the lobby and still having no idea what *It's a Wonderful Life* was about. The auditorium was sold out, but we were able to find two seats fairly close to the stage. Mine was at the end of the row and, as fate would have it, sitting directly across the aisle from me was Karolyn Grimes. She played ZuZu Bailey, the daughter of George Bailey, the film's main character. Right behind Karolyn was Jimmy Hawkins who, in the movie, played her brother, Tommy Bailey.

Remember, this was the first time in my life that I would be seeing this classic picture. By chance, I ended up sitting an aisle away from two of its stars, although at the time I sat down, I had no idea who they were.

Also intriguing to me was the fact that I was the one Walter invited to see this movie. He had plenty of other people that he could have asked. Coincidentally, at that time, I had been going through a period in my life where I was questioning my purpose. Every day, I started on my knees praying to God to help me do His will. Interestingly, I was regularly being put in situations of helping people better their lives. You'd think that that would make me happy—which, in reality, it did. However, since *my* own dreams had not yet come true, I constantly pondered the purpose of my existence.

The pre-screening festivities, including a question-and-answer session about the history of the movie and its characters, lasted about thirty minutes. Then suddenly the theatre went dark, music began playing, and up went the curtain. I became extremely excited, like a young child on Christmas morning. Finally, I was going to see this classic film for the very first time in my life.

Wikipedia's description of the movie says:

> *The film stars James Stewart as George Bailey, a man who has given up his dreams in order to help others, and whose imminent suicide on Christmas Eve brings about the intervention of his guardian angel, Clarence Odbody. Clarence shows George all the lives he has touched and how different life in his community of Bedford Falls would be like if he had never been born.*

Perhaps you are like I was and haven't already seen this movie. There was an incident involving the theft of a large sum of George Bailey's money. Hence, he was in jeopardy of losing his business, bringing him a sense of doom. George began questioning why he was even alive. Then, many of the townspeople that he helped throughout his life happily pitched in and gave George the money he needed to pay his debt and save his business. He now had a new outlook and felt that perhaps his life *did* have purpose.

While watching the movie, I had plenty of thoughts going through my mind. First, I was thinking about where my life was at that time.

I then considered the feelings that George Bailey had regarding his life and how he and I had followed similar paths. Furthermore, I wondered how I always seem to get the messages I need at the exact time they'll have the most impact on me.

As the movie ended, I now knew who Karolyn Grimes and Jimmy Hawkins were. I was honored to have sat so close to them during my first viewing of *It's A Wonderful Life.*

Walking over to Karolyn, I began a conversation with her, and she was just as nice as could be. Interestingly, Karolyn told me that she had not seen the film even once until she was almost forty years old. Despite that, as of that evening, she claimed she had now seen the movie nearly five hundred times! Almost as soon as Karolyn finished that comment, a mob of other theatre-goers gathered around us. I took a couple of pictures with Karolyn and then went to visit Jimmy, who was equally cordial.

It was now nearly eleven o'clock—time for Walter and I to head back to Studio City. Walking out of the theatre, I checked my cellphone and listened to two new voice messages. They were from the owners of the damaged car, Peter and Marcy, who thanked me for leaving a note on their vehicle, and asked me to call them the next day.

Crossing the street to the parking garage, I told Walter about those messages. He responded with some kind thoughts about my actions. My eyes began to water as I listened to him. I had simply done what I felt was right. Getting into Walter's car, it was time to go home and reminisce about the memorable evening.

The following morning, I called Peter and Marcy and shared with them details of the accident, including a description of the driver and the minivan. I also told them about the pictures I took of the vehicle's license plate and damage. The couple then shared some thoughts about the minor scrapes on the paint of the right rear quarter panel of their hatchback. They said that if the driver of the minivan had simply left a note, they probably would have thanked him for his honesty and considered it just "one of those things." Since he didn't do so, Peter and Marcy figured they would accept my help and have their car repaired.

Early the next day, their insurance adjuster called me and I told him what I had witnessed. I also mentioned the pictures that I took of the minivan's damage and emailed copies to him. Assuredly, I was confident that the adjuster would be able to find the minivan's driver. Then, as it should be, Peter and Marcy would have their car newly painted.

A few days after our conversation, they sent me a very nice email. It read:

> *Thanks so much – we stop & help when we see an*
> *accident & have sometimes felt we were the only ones*
> *around – you are restoring our faith in (most of)*
> *humanity. We're taking the car in for estimate Mon &*
> *to schedule work. Soon this will be a thing of the past!*
> *Have a wonderful holiday season! Marcy & Peter.*

On the day I went to see *It's A Wonderful Life*, I had asked God what I could do to be of maximum service for Him and my fellows. My answer showed up loud and clear later that night in the parking garage.

If you really fulfill the royal law according to the Scripture,
"You shall love your neighbor as yourself," you do well.
[NKJV Bible James 2:8]

---

* * *

TEAR-FILLED THANK YOU

After Peter and Marcy had their car repaired, I received another email from them:

> *Hey Rob – wanted to share the blog post I gave to "Let's Talk Nation" yesterday – you were the inspiration! If you're willing to share it, please email your mailing address – want to send a little something your way for the holidays. Thanks again for everything! Marcy.*

I sent Marcy my information. A few days later, tears fell from my eyes when I received a wonderful gift card in the mail from her and Peter. It was to their favorite place, one of the area's nicest movie theatres.

This is the blog post that Marcy—who is a professional writer—gave to "Let's Talk Nation:"

PAGING GEORGE BAILEY
by Marcy Rothenburg

We saw Frank Capra's "It's A Wonderful Life" last night.

In honor of the movie's 70th anniversary, the Academy of Motion Picture Arts & Sciences hosted a sell-out crowd at a $5-per-ticket screening at the Samuel L. Goldwyn Theatre in Beverly Hills. There is no better deal in movie-going America.

Heartened in this difficult political season by the film's message—that people like George Bailey, who choose to devote their lives to helping others, can win out over the greedy, venal Mr. Potters of the universe—we headed back to the parking garage with our daughter and son-in-law to begin the drive home.

Only to discover a nasty paint scrape on the driver's side rear bumper of our car, and a business-card note stuck in the driver's door window. It wasn't from the driver who'd hit our car, but from a Good Samaritan who'd witnessed the accident and captured photos on his phone of the offending driver's license plate and damage to his minivan.

Which, our Angel Clarence of the evening reported, the guy had spent ten minutes trying to buff out before moving to another parking space— presumably so we wouldn't see the damage on his vehicle if we returned to our car before he did.

I spent the rest of the night torn between feelings of anger at the selfish coward who'd hit and run, and gratitude for the willingness of a stranger to take action—even as scenes from Capra's masterpiece swirled in my head.

We talked to our witness today. He's sending along the photos and said he'd be happy to talk to our insurance company about what he saw. I'm grateful that he cares enough to get involved—and grateful that the visual evidence he has given us may help us recoup the cost of repairing our car.

But I'm still furious at someone who could watch THAT movie and not feel compelled to do the right thing. How could he watch George Bailey give up his own dreams to take care of his neighbors, while actively shirking responsibility for his own actions? How could he drive off and leave someone else holding the financial bag for the wrong he had done?

I probably won't get to ask him that question. Hopefully, our insurance company will identify him through the license plate photo and deal directly with him and his insurer on our behalf.

But if I did have the chance, I'd challenge his ill will. And tell him to watch the movie again—and again and again—until he has finally learned his lesson.

After reading that blog post, I was filled with varied emotions and, once again, I had plenty of tears rolling down my face.

Perhaps it would have been easier for me to simply walk away from the accident that I witnessed. I could have merely shaken my head in disbelief at the minivan driver's actions and gone into the theatre to enjoy the movie. Most likely, though, it would have preoccupied me throughout the entire film. I may have missed my opportunity to truly enjoy such a wonderful experience—and I might even have missed the moral of the film's story.

So, was it really just coincidence that Walter chose me to see that movie? Was it simply coincidence that I ended up being in a position to help some fellow human beings only hours after asking God for such an opportunity? Was it purely coincidence that the movie delivered an impactful message showing me that my life *already* had purpose (even as I was waiting for my dreams to materialize)?

Indeed, just like George Bailey, I discovered that my life *did* have purpose, and I would imagine that many other viewers of this timeless classic feel the same way.

CHAPTER 8: AN ADVENTURE BEYOND IMAGINATION

MY life has been filled with many incredible moments, but what I experienced in the events that I will share throughout this chapter were far beyond anything I could have ever imagined.

In Chapter 1, I mentioned that I had been a TV shopping host for nearly fifteen years—after which, I tried my hand at pitching products in front of live audiences at several fairs in California. During a recent July, I had an opening in my work schedule. On my friend Mikey's Facebook page, I noticed that he secured a sales position at the upcoming fair in Orange County, which began in a couple of days. So I texted him to let him know that I was available to work if anyone needed help. Usually all the booths would be fully staffed by now, but you never know.

On Friday, the first day of the fair, I received a welcome text from Mikey telling me to call Susan, a vendor he knew, ASAP, as she unexpectedly needed another salesperson. When I contacted her a few minutes later, Susan said that the available position was to sell massage pillows—reportedly a popular product. I had never seen those pillows before, but had no reason to doubt her claim. Susan then told me that her booth would be covered by another person that weekend. I could start working on the following Wednesday when the fair re-opened, as it was closed on Monday and Tuesday. Jackpot! You grind through long hours at such events but can make a handsome amount of money.

Upon getting what I believed was great news, I immediately called my then ninety-two-year-old spiritual friend, Tony, in Los Angeles to tell him of my good fortune. Expressing my excitement, I could sense him shaking his head back and forth on the other end of the telephone. I shared with Tony that I'd be selling massage pillows, a popular product, and by the end of the fair, I should be taking home a nice windfall of cash. In a composed voice full of wisdom, Tony responded that, though he was excited about my new opportunity, he said that I would not be making very much money. I quickly asked him where he got that idea and told him that he was gravely mistaken.

Tony calmly stated that he was being given a message from the Holy Spirit who told him that my job at the fair was simply to spend a month blessing people. Continuing on, Tony adamantly conveyed that I was not to worry about making money, and shouldn't be surprised each day to earn only a few dollars. Assuredly, this wasn't what I was hoping to hear from him.

I was puzzled by Tony's thought process. After all, I'd be working at a fair in one of the richest counties in America selling a popular product—so, surely, I was destined to bring home the big bucks...wasn't I?

But what if Tony was right? What if I spend a month working sixty-hour weeks and make hardly any money, but instead, simply put smiles on strangers' faces? What would that be like?

I've previously mentioned that I start every morning on my knees, asking God to help me to do His will and not mine. What if His will for me was to learn how to trust Him on a much higher level—to believe that He had something planned for me that would be immeasurably *greater* than a big paycheck?

Trust in the Lord with all your heart,
And lean not on your own understanding,
In all your ways acknowledge Him,
And he shall direct your paths.
[NKJV Bible Proverbs 3 5-6]

Now that I had the gig at the fair, I quickly called my friend Patrick to ask if I could stay with him at his condo. He lives in Huntington Beach, only about ten minutes from the fair grounds. Upon my asking, Patrick graciously said that I could stay with him for the month, which would give us some time to catch up on life. That was awesome, as our schedules had previously kept us from spending time together during the past few years. I would also escape the stress of driving on the crowded LA freeways, as my normal ride to the fair was more than an hour, even without any traffic.

The following Wednesday morning, it was time to get to work, so I showed up at the fair on time as scheduled. After settling into my booth, I was feeling excited and was ready to start earning some cash.

Before the doors opened, I strolled over to say hi to Mikey, whose booth was in the next aisle over from me. Picking up on my excitement, Mikey caught me a bit off guard, though, when instead of mirroring my expectations for a big pay day, he immediately told me not to expect much in terms of sales this month. Mikey stated that the massage pillows that I would be selling—although great products—had been sold at numerous events during the past six years.

Say what? Susan hadn't mentioned that part to me when I was hired. From my previous experience, I knew that people attend fairs looking for the *newest* gadgets and inventions, so having to sell older inventory this month was a real bummer. Mikey had originally wanted me to contact Susan for this job because he knew that she had plenty of *new* products to sell, but other workers were already assigned to those items. He wanted me to get my foot in the door with Susan because of the prospect of good future earnings. Mikey was thinking of me for the long term, and had my best interests in mind.

Nonetheless, I was discouraged when Mikey seemingly echoed Tony's previous sentiment that I wouldn't be getting rich this month. I doubted Tony when he predicted my lack of earnings at this fair, but after talking with Mikey, I started to think that maybe Tony was right. Perhaps my ONLY job this month would be to bless people. What, though, would that really mean? I had no clue.

Returning to my booth, I spent time getting acclimated to the massage pillows, as I was still determined to bring in as much cash as possible. Yet, I quickly learned some not-so-exciting, but valuable, information as fairgoers began stopping by to talk to me. Adding to my dismay, they shared stories of having already bought those pillows a year or two before and how much they still enjoyed them. That was nice to hear for their sakes; however, it wasn't helping me to put any money in my pocket today.

During my first week at the fair, I worked sixty hours but made less than four hundred dollars. That's obviously far below minimum wage and, unfortunately, it was a commission-only job. Upon adding up my small windfall and feeling quite frustrated, I called Tony to share my misery. Again, I could sense his head shaking on the other end of the phone. He responded that it was more money than I had when the week started. Then he reiterated that my sole job at the fair was *simply to bless people*. Tony could not understand why I was in such shock over making so little cash.

Throughout the next two weeks, I experienced similar monetary results. Each night after work, I would make the short ride back to Patrick's house, where I was able to talk about my challenges at the fair and the growing sense that my life's purpose was again in question. Patrick would patiently listen to my griping for a while, but then he'd recount stories from the past twenty years reminding me of the number of people that I have inspired and helped. Sadly, I hadn't remembered any of them.

These conversations proved to be invaluable, as they appeared to be more confirmation from God that my perception is not always my reality.

Halfway through the third week of the fair, I had another interesting experience. There was a twenty-nine-year-old black woman, Tracy, working in the booth next to mine. Surprisingly, with no one else around, she yelled to me, "You're a Christian, aren't you?"

I responded, "Yes."

Then I walked over to ask her what I was doing to give her that impression. Tracy told me that it was the way I talked to people, and how I treated my customers. Even more, she stated it was the way that I *blessed* them. Seriously?

I immediately went outside and called Tony to tell him what just happened. He broke out laughing, and then reminded me that I was doing exactly what God wanted from me. I was lost, though, as to exactly how I was blessing people. Nonetheless, I went back inside to talk to more prospects.

Two days later on Sunday, I had a similar encounter. Richard, a seventy-five-year-old Asian gentleman, owned the booth on the *other* side of me. Before the fair opened that day, he hurried over to give me some encouragement. Richard shared that he had been watching me closely over the past three weeks and saw that—while I wasn't making much money—I was *blessing* people on a daily basis. Unbelievable! I nearly fell to the ground.

Our conversation continued for almost an hour. Throughout that time, Richard assured me not to be discouraged by my lack of sales. He emphasized that I was surely doing God's work and I should continue to do so because I would receive my reward from Him.

Hello, what's happening here?

I had worked at the fair for three weeks—twelve hours per day, five days per week—trying to sell massage pillows. My efforts brought in barely any cash. Then, within a couple of days, I had a pair of incredible experiences. Two people—both from different cultures and nearly fifty years apart in age—whom I'd never met before, each told me something profoundly similar. They both said that they had been enjoying themselves watching the way I worked and continually blessed people. Still, I had no idea what I was actually doing that people would consider a blessing.

That night, after my conversation with Richard, I drove to Patrick's house and told him what happened. I explained to him my challenge of not knowing what I was doing that others saw as a blessing to people. Patrick's response caught me completely off guard. He said that perhaps I was simply just being me, and my enthusiastic spirit was what brought joy to people. That was certainly not something I was expecting to hear.

Tears instantly swelled in my eyes as Patrick's words brought back some painful memories for me. I thought of the eighteen years that I spent wearing a toupée so that I could look "acceptable" to the world. Now, it was nearly fifteen years since I stopped putting on my fake hair. Bald is beautiful! Patrick reminded me that in God's eyes, all I ever had to be was me. That was good enough.

"For we are God's masterpiece.
He has created us anew in Christ Jesus,
so we can do the good things he planned for us long ago."
[NLT Bible Ephesians 2:10]

There's something interesting that I've discovered about myself. When life's not going my way, I start looking at what it is that I'm doing wrong. Not that I am actually off-track in any way.

Wise friends have pointed out that God has a plan for me and a lull in my career activity does not mean that I'm on the wrong path. Instead, He's setting me up for something more than I could imagine. That was proven to me mere moments after Richard and I finished our conversation earlier that day.

* * *

MY CHOICE...ALASKA

A few weeks prior to beginning my work at the fair, I answered an internet ad posted by a company in Alaska looking for a naturalist on their small cruise ship. They responded, saying that the position had already been filled and to check back next year if I was still interested.

Less than an hour after Richard had spoken with me, I received a call from Jack, the owner and captain of that ship. He said that the position had again become available, and asked me if I was still interested in working for him. I said yes, but requested more information. Jack then stated that he had looked at my credentials but, unfortunately, didn't feel that he could pay me what I was worth. He did, however, share that I would get a complimentary room on his ship, free meals, and roundtrip airfare from Los Angeles to Juneau.

Jack next mentioned that he would fly me to Juneau on August 15. Perfect, as that was two days after the fair closed. I'd be working on three cruises through the end of September. This would give me the opportunity to journey around southeast Alaska—something I had wanted to do for a couple of years. Two weeks later, in October, we'd begin the first of two trips on the Columbia and Snake Rivers traveling through Oregon, Washington, and Idaho—three more places that I'd never been. I was already committed to another project in Kentucky during the first week of October, which fit in nicely before Jack would need me later that month.

As there wasn't a big paycheck involved, I nearly passed on Jack's offer. After all, I'd been working for virtually nothing the past several weeks—plus, I would have more profitable opportunities available after the fair ended.

At the time, I was at a place in my life that allowed me to explore new experiences. Also, I had never been on a cruise ship before. So I decided against making a bigger paycheck and, instead, chose to take Jack's offer: five cruises, meals, and presumably sensational sightseeing in some of the most picturesque places on the planet.

Once my call with Jack ended, I phoned Tony to divulge all the good news that I had received throughout the day. He reacted with a joyous laughter in his voice and was ecstatic about what I shared with him. When our fifteen-minute conversation ended, I went back to my booth with a renewed vigor and spirit.

After work that night, I was outside the fair waiting in line for the shuttle bus to bring me to my car. A gentleman came and stood alongside me, and asked how my day had gone. I mentioned my lack of sales and asked him what he sold. Reaching into a bag, the man pulled out a small version of the New Testament, handed it to me, and said that he didn't sell anything. The gentleman told me that he worked for the Gideons, passing out mini-Bibles at the fair. I thanked him for my gift and introduced myself. He likewise introduced himself, saying that his name was *Jeremiah.*

I instantly recalled from the Bible that Jeremiah was one of the major prophets who authored several books of the Old Testament. Could this be? Seriously, Lord, this cannot be happening!

The shuttle arrived and moments later I was at my car. Before getting in, I called Tony to tell him of my experience with Jeremiah. Again, I received an earful of his joyful mirth, as Tony is my Bible expert and understood the "coincidence." I tell people that Tony can quote the Bible with his eyes closed, and the mention of that incident between Jeremiah and me verified to Tony what he already knew— that I was indeed doing what God had asked of me.

* * *

A WELL-CRAFTED PLAN

A week after meeting Jeremiah, my month of blessing people was over—as the fair came to an end—but not until ten o'clock at night. Then I had to dismantle my booth, and by the time I got home, it was nearly two o'clock in the morning. I only had this one day to get ready to fly to Juneau, to begin my first cruise with Jack. Fortunately, I didn't need to bring much because he said that he'd provide me with shirts and jackets. So, within a few hours of waking up, I was packed and ready to go to Alaska. Perhaps *there* I would enjoy what Tony and Richard had predicted from my work at the fair, that is, a special reward from God.

There are no nonstop flights to Juneau from southern California, so I had to change planes at Sea-Tac (Seattle-Tacoma) airport. While there, I went to a gift shop to buy some water. Grabbing a bottle, I turned around and was immediately taken aback. Literally twelve inches in front of me was a display rack with a book directly at my eyeline titled, *I Am: 40 Reasons to Trust God.* Right next to it was another book titled, *In Alaska with God on the Adventure of a Lifetime.* Amazing!

Here I was ready to embark on an opportunity as I never had before. Now, having seen those books, I believed that God was making it clear that He was definitely orchestrating my upcoming adventures.

Leaving Seattle, I then flew to Juneau. I arrived there just after noon, which gave me time to visit with friends that I hadn't seen in a few months, before meeting Jack on his ship at five o'clock. Once on board, I exchanged pleasantries with him and some of the staff. I was feeling a burst of excitement as I would soon be embarking on a new, and hopefully awesome, adventure.

Jack's ship holds thirty-two passengers and nine crew members. After putting my luggage in my cabin, I went to the back of the boat to check out the view. Bam! Only a few feet in front of me sat a mega-million-dollar ship named *Serenity.* How appropriate!

In most of the twelve-step meetings that I attend, we recite a portion of the *Serenity Prayer,* which was written by American theologian, Reinhold Niebuhr:

God grant me the Serenity to accept the things I cannot change,
courage to change the things I can,
and wisdom to know the difference.

Oddly enough, the vessel docked immediately to our right was named *Alaskan Story.* Seeing that boat along with the one named

Serenity caused me to remember the two books that I had seen a few hours earlier in Seattle. Consequently, I felt that same clear message that I did then. God was no doubt directing this adventure.

I enjoyed an evening of dinner with a couple of crew members and then settled into my cabin. The next morning, I woke up before the rest of the staff and walked to a twelve-step meeting. Afterwards, I headed back to help with final preparations on our ship. We'd begin cruising at six o'clock that evening—which would be my first such journey ever—and as much as I was excited, I also did not know what to expect.

My position was officially titled "Cruise Host." Thus, part of my job was to entertain our new passengers, starting at two in the afternoon at the Alaska State Museum in downtown Juneau. There, I made sure that everyone who would be joining us on the cruise was in town. With that accomplished, most of our guests then spent about an hour at the museum before taking a leisurely walk to explore the area.

By 4:45 p.m., all our passengers were gathered together near the cruise ship docks, ready to head to our vessel. After I led them on the short walk there, some of the crew members greeted the guests and showed them to their cabins. Soon after, they all ventured upstairs to our lounge for cocktails and appetizers. At six o'clock sharp, Captain Jack sounded the horn—signaling the beginning of my first excursion around southeast Alaska.

The ensuing adventure over the next nine days was designed to encounter as much wildlife and gorgeous scenery as possible. Throughout the first three days, we enjoyed bright sunshine, breathtaking landscapes, and plenty of whale sightings. Our first three nights were spent anchored in peaceful coves. Late on day 4, we traveled to Petersburg, Alaska, a well-known salmon processing town of about thirty-six hundred residents. As soon as we pulled into the harbor, I noticed the boat directly in front of us. It was named

Puffin—which really caught my attention—as it reminded me of my late grandfather, Homer. He was an award-winning nature photographer. The license plate on his van was PUFFIN—his favorite bird.

Nearly every summer, Homer would drive from either New York or southern New England to Machias Seal Island, located off the coast between Maine and Canada. Besides hanging out with the locals, he would take pictures of the vast number of puffins. Seeing that boat next to us in Petersburg, I believed that Homer was watching over me as I experienced my first big-time nature adventure.

Now docked in Petersburg, Jack told me that I'd be escorting our passengers the next day both to the local museum and on a hike through a nature trail. However, he claimed that he didn't know where I would find either place. Having never been to Petersburg, I obviously did not have any idea where I'd be going either, so I decided to explore the town that night.

Walking up the dock to the main street, I strolled a short distance before going into a local book store. There was an older teenage boy at the counter, and I asked him how to get to the museum. He stated that he wasn't too familiar with the area, as his father and he only recently moved to Petersburg from northern California—although he did offer to look up the directions on the internet.

After the teenager found the directions, I thanked him and introduced myself. He then told me that his name was *Noah* (seriously?) and his father had just become the head pastor at a church in town.

So, first I meet *Jeremiah*, who hands out mini-Bibles. Then I get help from *Noah*, whose father is a pastor.

Exiting the book store, I immediately called my friend, Tony, who—upon hearing this story—once again broke out laughing, finding it funny that I was the only one surprised by such events. After our call ended, I walked to the museum. Someone there gave me directions to the entrance of the nature trail and I ventured over to see it. Now having the information that I needed to guide our passengers on a walk the following day, I headed back to our ship. Once there, I joined the guests for dinner.

Later that night, I sat on the back of our vessel staring at the boat, *Puffin*, while talking to my grandfather in the sky. The next morning, as the sun came up, I took a picture of that boat. I wanted to keep track of all these interesting "coincidences" that were happening on my journey.

When the passengers and I finished breakfast, I guided them on our hike. In addition to the fabulous scenery, we noticed plenty of evidence that bears had been in the area; unfortunately, however, we didn't see any actual bears.

A visit to the local museum was our next stop. There we learned about the history of Petersburg, a fishing village of Norwegian heritage, famed for its significance in the salmon canning industry. The city is home to nearly seven hundred commercial fishermen. Leaving the museum, our guests had the opportunity to do some shopping in town before returning to our ship.

Heading out to sea from Petersburg, we cruised around southeast Alaska during the next few days, seeing numerous humpback whales and witnessing a couple of glaciers calving. (That's the natural breaking off of large pieces of ice.) In a secluded cove named Pavlof Harbor, we watched five brown bears fishing for salmon. That was spectacular! Jack also sailed us to Brothers Island, which was filled with hundreds of sea lions. We then visited the Five Finger Lighthouse, located north of Petersburg and south of Juneau. It opened in 1902 and was the first U.S. government lighthouse in Alaska. We definitely enjoyed an exciting and educational trip before docking back in Juneau.

The next morning, it was time to say goodbye to our guests. My first official cruise around southeast Alaska was over and I was thrilled to have had that experience. Our crew and I then spent a day and a half cleaning our ship to ready it for the next trip. As routine as all that preparation was, I could not have imagined just what treasures were in store for us during the next nine-day adventure.

To begin with, we encountered rare sightings of large groups of humpback whales *bubblenet feeding.* (A unique surface feeding behavior of humpback whales often done in groups.) Then, while again at Pavlof Harbor, we went kayaking and witnessed thirteen brown bears, most of which were fishing in front of a giant, thundering waterfall. Three small cubs were sitting on the shore watching mama catch some fresh salmon for their dinner. At the same time, a sneaky adult male brown bear tried to snatch one of the cubs, but the alarmed mama flew out of the water and chased him off. That incident was as exciting as it was frightening and definitely made great dinnertime conversation among our passengers.

Seeing these types of events on television is one thing, but you cannot feel their true magnificence until you're witnessing them in person with your own eyes. Watching those bears in their natural environment was absolutely incredible.

* * *

MIRACLE ON ICE

Even more amazing are the times when you happen to come upon a manifestation of nature so unusual that there is no logical explanation as to how it could have happened. That's exactly what I encountered the following day on our return to Dawes Glacier, where we had visited only five days earlier on our last cruise.

There was an enormous amount of "ice pack" (mini-icebergs floating in front of the glacier), which is typical evidence of a lot of recent calving. That was surely exacerbated by the current string of sunny days and above-average temperatures which warmed the water around the glacier. Being extremely dense in composition, pieces of an ice pack can cause plenty of damage to a smaller boat's hull, like ours. Many similar ships wouldn't risk trying to make their way through such an ice field, but we had an adventurous crew.

Determined to give our passengers the best possible experience, Captain Jack and the first mate decided to maneuver our vessel through nearly three miles of that very thick ice pack. (This is much like trying to drive your vehicle through a crowded freeway at rush hour.) After gingerly guiding our boat across the giant ice field for nearly an hour, we arrived at Dawes Glacier. Jack parked in front of it, keeping us about a half mile away in case any larger pieces of ice were to fall off the glacier and into the water. They could cause tremendous swells, which might seriously rock our boat and possibly harm our guests. Since the glacier was so huge, even at that distance, we could still see its intimate details and formations.

As the frigid breeze coming off of Dawes Glacier blew around us, many of the passengers and I stood outside on our ship's bow (the front of the boat). The sun glistened down upon the glacier with its deep blue color and jagged edges along the front and top. Finding a great place to stand without hindering our guests, I began taking pictures. With my naked eye I could see that the front of the glacier had changed dramatically since our recent visit. I was able to verify this by looking at photographs I had previously taken.

After about fifteen minutes, I decided to walk to the upper deck to see if I could get a different perspective, and perhaps see something that I couldn't from my current position. Arriving at my new higher location, about twenty feet above where I had been, I found myself all alone. Looking down at the passengers on the bow, I saw that for whatever reason, they were all focused on the right-hand side of the glacier. Possibly, they heard some cracking sounds, which generally precede a calving—our purpose for going to Dawes Glacier.

Since the guests were all staring in one direction, I decided to keep my eyes focused that way as well. After ten minutes of not hearing any cracking or seeing even a small piece of ice falling, I started to scan my camera across the front of the glacier from right to left. As I crossed the mid-way point, I was taken aback by what I saw. At once, I lowered the camera to verify my discovery. It looked to me like there was something carved into the glacier. My eyes seemed to perceive a masterfully sculpted, life-sized figure with its arms outstretched. The longer I gazed at it, the more it looked like an angel.

The detail seemed so clear, that even after a couple of double-takes, my mind questioned the probability of such a sight. I began taking pictures of it at a feverish pace to capture the sculpture from various angles—trying to include as many of its details as possible. I also wanted to get the greatest number of photos of that figure before any calving occurred in the area, which would surely destroy it.

Amidst the chaos of thousands of jagged hunks of ice was this serenely angelic figure, improbably fashioned, and perhaps within even moments of our arrival. I was absolutely astounded, especially having witnessed the incredible amount of ice pack that we had to wallow through to get to the glacier—proving that there had been a tremendous amount of calving over the past few days. Certainly, no human being could be responsible for this heavenly figure; one would have to climb the glacier, secure herself to the front of it, and spend hours carving the ice—creating what appeared to be a perfect piece of art. This was beyond belief. Right in front of me was a true miracle on ice!

Something else was very intriguing to me. I noticed that while the entire glacier's ice was intensely blue in color—the "angel" appeared in white—seemingly illuminated by its own natural spotlight. The sun was shining upon the full face of the glacier, and normally the entirety of the formation would appear in the same blue hue, with minor variations due to the density of the ice. Therefore, it was all the more striking that this angel emerged from its surroundings so distinctly in its own white brilliance.

To my eyes, the image was so perfectly clear. Knowing that the glacier had seen a lot of recent calving, the only way that the figure could have come to be was through a phenomenal act.

Ecstatic to have numerous photos of the discovery, I rushed down to the lower deck to share my inconceivable find with our passengers. Going from person to person, about twenty in all, I showed them my pictures and pointed out the perceived figure on the glacier. I was shocked to hear that only a few of them said that they *kind of* saw it, some seemed either confused or preoccupied, and still others looked at me like I was crazy.

It was strikingly odd to me that even though I could still see it clearly from my now lower angle, no one else seemed able to detect the angel in the ice. That completely baffled me. It stood out so intently to me. Conceivably, the passengers were so hoping to see a calving of the glacier that they could not devote their attention to anything else. Maybe some were not interested in looking at what I was describing. Perhaps, even, it wasn't meant for them to see.

Having little success sharing what I believed could never be experienced again, I rushed back to the upper deck and snapped a few more pictures. I then paused, staring with fascination at my new friend, the angel on ice. Tears began rolling down my face as I was hit with the overwhelming feeling that God was communicating his presence to me so powerfully...as only He could. In my mind and heart, I had no doubt that God was responsible for that wondrous creation.

Completely drained from both the frigid temperature and all the emotional energy spent experiencing that angel, I went to my cabin and put my camera away. Then I laid on my bed for a few minutes, with more tears rolling down my face, and began thinking about how extraordinary the previous several weeks had been for me. Without a doubt, everything had fallen perfectly into place—since I first sent Mikey the text about working at the Orange County Fair, to ending up in Alaska, to me being in front of this glacier—witnessing the unimaginable. There had to be something at work much greater than just a series of "coincidences" that was responsible for all of those events.

We spent a bit over an hour at Dawes Glacier. Crew members had handed out hot chocolate to our guests who waited expectantly for a major calving. Unfortunately, to their great dismay, there was no such event, and I felt sorry that they didn't get to see the spectacle that they had hoped to witness.

As much as I would have enjoyed seeing a huge calving, myself, I feel fortunate to have experienced something even more magnificent and unparalleled. I had captured images that no one else ever had or likely ever would—both with my camera and my heart.

* * *

SIGNS, SIGNS, SIGNS

After watching several small calvings of Dawes Glacier, we returned to Petersburg, where we happened to dock next to a boat named *Westerly*. This was more evidence to me that Homer was watching me from above. He passed away in Westerly, Rhode Island.

Staying the night in Petersburg, we fueled up our vessel in the morning, then were entertained over the next few days by cruising into more of the secluded areas of southeast Alaska. Throughout that time, we enjoyed stunning landscapes and wildlife, including bald eagles, sea otters, bears, and whales. Then we returned to Juneau for the last time of the summer and bid *bon voyage* to our guests.

Having cleaned the ship, our crew had one last day off before heading out on a fourteen-day journey from Alaska to Seattle. Jack flew back east and would meet up with us several days later in Ketchikan. Captain Brennan was set to guide us until then. I was tremendously excited about this upcoming excursion. Along the way, we'd be stopping in two cities that I'd been wanting to visit—Ketchikan and Wrangell.

A few days into that trip, we arrived in Wrangell and were treated to a nearly five-hour jet boat ride on the Stikine River. It's approximately four hundred miles long, running from British

Columbia, Canada, to Wrangell. We certainly didn't travel the entire length of the river, but it was an awesome boat ride.

Along our route, we saw numerous species of wildlife, including seals, sea lions, and bald eagles. The highlight of our day was seeing some huge icebergs and the Shakes Glacier. The area—with its gorgeous mountains, waterfalls, and foliage—was one of the most picturesque regions that you could imagine. Famed naturalist John Muir explored Wrangell in 1879 and was extremely impressed, calling the Stikine River "a Yosemite one hundred miles long."

Three days after leaving Wrangell, with the rarity of sunshine above us, we visited the normally very wet city of Ketchikan. Its annual rainfall total is nearly thirteen feet. (Yes, I said *thirteen feet* of rain *per year*). Comparably, the average yearly rainfall in Los Angeles is only about fifteen inches. The nice weather in Ketchikan allowed our passengers some time to enjoy the beauty of the city.

For the crew, it was our last opportunity to fuel up, clean the boat, and buy any necessary food and supplies. We'd be spending the upcoming three days cruising nonstop through Canadian waters. Captain Jack had returned and he, Captain Brennan, and first mate Tommy would be driving the boat 24/7 until we reached the San Juan Islands in northern Washington.

Traveling through Canada proved to be incredible as we enjoyed bright blue skies, as well as some of the most sensational sunrises and sunsets that I had ever seen. We were also able to watch a pod of orcas put on quite a show, as well as enjoy some Dall's porpoises swimming alongside of our ship for several miles.

Once through Canadian waters, our next stop was in the San Juan Islands at the very intimate and historic town of Roche Harbor. This was the perfect place to dock for a night after spending a harrowing three days without being able to get off our ship. Talk about cabin fever!

After dinner, I was standing in our lounge talking with one of our passengers, Jim. He asked me what I would be doing for the rest of the year as it was now almost the middle of October, and we only had two trips left on the Columbia River. Before answering Jim, I happened to look out the window over my left shoulder and, once more, was amazed. There was a very exotic boat docked next to us named *NO WORRIES*—seemingly another sign that God was continuing to watch over me.

Pausing for a moment, I gently shook my head in wonderment of the "coincidence" between the timing of Jim's question and my noticing the name on that boat. I then looked back at him and answered, "I'm not sure. God hasn't given me my next assignment yet—but apparently He has it all under control."

Halfway through the following day, we left the San Juan Islands and headed to Seattle where, about six hours later, our fourteen-day journey from Juneau ended. However, that would not be my last trip of the year with Captain Jack. Three weeks later we'd take two more cruises up and down the Columbia and Snake Rivers through Oregon, Washington, and Idaho.

During our time off, I flew back to Los Angeles, and then to Kentucky, where I emceed at a convention at the Louisville Fair Grounds. The event was a fast four days total of flying and working.

Now back in Los Angeles, I flew to Portland, Oregon, and then was captivated throughout a scenic two-hour car ride to Astoria, the oldest town in the Pacific Northwest. There, we'd begin the final two cruises of the season at the mouth of the Columbia River. After several days of preparing our boat, the next group of passengers arrived, and I was excited to begin my first-ever journey through this historic region.

Before sailing off, though, we spent most of the morning on a bus tour, visiting various places of interest around Astoria. Most notably, the Maritime Museum and the "Astoria Column," a local tower with a 164-step spiral staircase leading to an outside perch overlooking the area's beautiful landscape. This was a great start to our seven-day adventure, and the passengers were eagerly anticipating our forthcoming expedition.

We enjoyed lunch on our ship; then, in mid-afternoon we left the harbor in Astoria and headed up "the Mighty Columbia" River. Over the next several days, we stopped for various short bus excursions—including visits to Mount St. Helens, Maryhill Museum, Bonneville Dam, and Multnomah Falls.

Five days into our journey, we connected with the Snake River, which we traveled to our final destination in Clarkston, Washington. While there, we took a jet boat ride into Hells Canyon, a challenging section of water that flows between Washington, Oregon, and Idaho. During that ride, we were able to see some bighorn sheep, great blue herons, and bald eagles. There were also a number of mule deer and wild turkeys. It was a great way to end a very invigorating cruise.

The next day, our passengers were driven by bus to their flights home, leaving out of the Spokane Airport in northeastern Washington. I joined them on the two-hour ride before I spent the night in an area hotel. The following morning, our bus driver and I returned to the airport, where we picked up our last group of guests for the season. This final cruise would last nine days and head back down the Snake and Columbia Rivers, eventually docking in Astoria.

There was an empty passenger cabin on the upper level of our ship, so I decided to stay there. On our next-to-last night of cruising on the Columbia River, we docked in the small town of Washougal, Washington. When we arrived there, my room happened to face the marina housing other boats, but since it was dark, I didn't notice much around us.

Early the next morning, I went for a walk along the Washougal shoreline. When I returned to my cabin, I opened the window to let in the crisp autumn air. As I did, I was taken aback one more time.

Staring straight at me was a small boat named *Serenity*. Tears filled my eyes as I recalled that when I first arrived in Juneau, there was another ship that was also named *Serenity*.

My best guess is that these were not mere coincidences; rather, God was telling me that trusting in Him would be where I would find my peace and serenity. Furthermore, He would continue to reveal Himself to me in extraordinary ways—as He had already done repeatedly in the stories that I've shared throughout this book.

Perhaps my friend Tony was right all along—that my job during the Orange County Fair was not to sell a bunch of massage pillows, or make a ton of cash. Rather, for a month I was simply to do what God wanted of me—that is, to bless people. In similar fashion, as Richard had encouraged me, God would reward me handsomely for keeping my focus on serving others instead of worrying about my finances.

For this final leg of the journey, we cruised out from Washougal, enjoyed more of the area's beautiful landscapes, and ended our trip the following day in Astoria. Having explored this wondrous area of the Pacific Northwest was, for me, a tremendous experience—as were all five cruises that I've recounted throughout this chapter. They comprised an adventure that was truly beyond my imagination...and proved to be a most remarkable "paycheck."

CHAPTER 9: MASTERFULLY DESIGNED, PERFECTLY DELIVERED

This final chapter begins in April and ends in September. Along with providing me many memorable moments, this period also involved numerous challenging experiences that tested me emotionally and spiritually to a degree I can't recall previously in my life. There was often a palpable sense of struggle while watching continuous crew member conflicts, staying true to my beliefs, and even witnessing a man take his final breath.

Having had much success working with Captain Jack on those five previously mentioned cruises, he asked me to return for the following season, saying that he really enjoyed having my spirit on his ship. I accepted his offer.

The new season began with our vessel docked north of Seattle, in Everett, Washington. Over the winter months, some newer crew members had been there working on various aspects of our boat's maintenance. Still, when I arrived on April 2, plenty more work needed to be done. Our first cruise of the year would begin in less than a week and would take place around the San Juan Islands, just north of Everett.

After a vigorous effort by all of the crew to prepare our boat, that first trip went off without many issues. A few days later, we had another such cruise which was equally successful. It was now the middle of April, and Captain Jack docked our ship in La Conner, an intimate harbor—about two hours north of Seattle. He spent several days with us before flying back east to handle some personal business. Meanwhile, our crew made final adjustments to the engine, pumps, and other aspects of the vessel, a necessity before we headed to Alaska for the summer on May 1.

The main focus of my job was to create presentations to share with our passengers throughout the summer. So, each day for nearly a week, I did research on the internet at the town library. Although I always walked the two miles to get there, we had a company pickup truck to share amongst the crew. Yet, some of the crew acted as if it was their own personal vehicle and drove it wherever and whenever they wanted to—and I was left out.

Five days after Jack's departure, he called and said that all employees had to take the next three days off. The following morning at about seven o'clock, I went to the first mate and asked him if I could use the truck for half a day. His response was anything but friendly. Even though I was bothered by his answer, instead of arguing with him, I felt that my best decision was to leave our ship and let God handle my transportation dilemma.

IS IT GOD OR COINCIDENCE?

---

*"I have told you these things, so that in me you may have peace.
In this world you will have trouble. But take heart! I have
overcome the world."*
[NIV Bible John 16:33]

The sun was shining, and it was a beautiful spring morning. There was a twelve-step meeting that I had never been to, which began in an hour at eight o'clock and was only about a mile away. I could walk there and get some exercise. So, I put my sneakers on and headed out to make some new friends.

When I arrived at the meeting hall, only four other men were there. One of them, a man named Otis, had brought along his wonderful dog, Tucker. With just five of us attending the hour-long gathering, we all had time to share some of our life experiences. After the meeting, one of the men, Bob, asked if I would like a ride to a meeting the next day in Anacortes, saying it was about a twenty-minute ride from our ship. I told Bob that I would definitely take him up on his offer—a comment which Otis apparently overheard.

Sunday morning, Bob picked me up and drove me across the mile-long bridge connecting La Conner to Fidalgo Island en route to the meeting hall in the city of Anacortes, where we gathered with about seventy-five others. Halfway through the meeting, there was a short break. I casually turned around and, unbeknownst to me, Otis was sitting there. I said hi to him and we began talking. Otis told me that he normally didn't go to this meeting. However, he stated that I shared something at our encounter the day before that touched his heart, and he wanted to go there today to thank me. Wow, that had never happened to me before. I didn't know how to respond to him, except to say thank you.

As our conversation continued, I discussed my challenge of not being able to use the company truck. Otis asked me if having a vehicle for the rest of the week would help me. I said yes, so he invited me to come to his home later that day. Bob agreed to drive me there.

When Bob and I arrived at Otis's house, he introduced me to his lovely wife and gave us a tour of their property. The inquisitive canine, Tucker, followed our every move. After some refreshments, Otis took me outside to see his pickup truck and a soft-covered jeep in the driveway. He said that I was welcome to use either one of them for the week at no cost. Incredible! Again, I was lost for words, but felt tremendously grateful.

Earlier, on our ride to the meeting, I had seen plenty of hills in the area, so I chose the pickup because it had an automatic transmission. Otis gave me the keys and said not to worry about returning the truck to him. He would pick it up when he brought his wife to visit our ship the following Saturday. Amazing! Otis only knew me for a couple of hours, yet he gave me the use of such a valuable possession. Why would he do this for me?

(So this is how God took care of my transportation *dilemma* in the moment and, as came to light later on, it was part of a masterfully designed plan to bring a memorable close to a tragic event.)

The next day, Monday, I received another blessing when I drove Otis's truck to a meeting in Anacortes which I otherwise wouldn't have been able to attend. While there, I shared that Ketchikan, Alaska, would be our first stop when we began our cruise north in a few days. Immediately after the meeting, the day's leader, a woman named Crystal, introduced herself. She mentioned that she lived in Ketchikan for thirty-five years before moving to Anacortes. During her last twelve years in Ketchikan, Crystal worked as a tour guide. Hence, she offered to meet me on Friday afternoon and bring several photos that she'd taken of the city and share insightful stories that I could relate to our passengers. Jackpot! Despite a few challenges while preparing our ship, this season was starting off much better than I could have expected.

On Tuesday night, I drove to another meeting and talked about the recent blessings that had come my way. Afterwards, a lady introduced herself to me and said that she had been originally scheduled to be the leader at yesterday's meeting, but at the last minute, she'd had an emergency and had called Crystal to fill in for her. Interesting....

Early the following morning, I ventured off to another sober gathering, where I was pleasantly surprised to see Otis and Tucker. The loving canine checked out everyone in the room before hopping up on the bench where I was sitting. He laid his head on my right thigh—near my arthritic hip—and fell asleep. I absolutely love dogs, and felt wonderfully blessed by Tucker's friendship, which helped make the meeting very special for me.

Having Otis's truck provided me with the opportunity to intimately explore Anacortes. While doing so, one day I saw people on top of a hill overlooking the ocean. Driving around the local neighborhoods, I was able to make my way up to that spot—Cap Santé Park. There, I had a perfect view of the ocean and the gorgeous landscape below. I was awestruck by the sight—comprised of snow-capped mountains on neighboring islands, birds gliding on the wafting ocean breezes, and numerous people on sailboats enjoying afternoon cruises on the crystal blue waters.

The week passed in a flash and Saturday arrived. Several enjoyable days of using Otis's truck came to an end. He, his wife, and Tucker came to our ship for a tour and to take home his pickup. After having a look around my summer home and partaking in some lively conversation, we said our goodbyes. Tucker gave me a giant doggie smooch.

Sadness filled my heart and tears fell from my eyes as I watched my newfound friends head to their vehicles. Again, I wondered why I had been the beneficiary of Otis's generosity. Time would soon bring me the answer.

Later that day, Captain Jack, who had returned from back east, sailed our vessel and crew to Seattle, where three days later we would begin our first cruise of the season to Alaska. Pushing to finish some needed work, I didn't get to bed until after midnight. I thought that I would be able to sleep until at least eight o'clock on Sunday morning; instead, I was awakened by a text message at five o'clock. Grabbing my cellphone in frustration, I instantly saw that the message was from Otis. Reading it, tears began rolling down my face and my lack of sleep no longer bothered me. Otis wrote:

> *Rob, I thought I'd share with you that Tucker is a service dog. He is a comfort animal who senses illness and discomfort in others. It's a bit uncanny, but undeniable about his abilities. He (as you may have noticed) greets every person in meetings, and must connect with them: even if someone comes in late, he must greet them. He is very special and connected with you, I think, because of your hip. He consistently amazes us. We don't often put his service vest on him unless around large crowds, or somewhere special. Additionally, he will always remember you! Travel well new friend. God has surely blessed you!*

Yes, I was definitely feeling blessed having met my new friends, Otis, his wife, and Tucker. However, along with all the blessings that I'd received throughout this first month, I had to witness a lot of negative and unnecessary behavior (mostly a lack of respect and unity among our crew members). As a result, I was considering other options that I had for the summer. That said, I strongly felt that God wanted me on our ship for an important assignment—although what that was, I wasn't sure.

Our initial cruise to Alaska began on May 1 and lasted fourteen days before we reached Juneau. Five days into our trip, we were set to stop in Ketchikan. A few hours before arriving there, I did a presentation about the city using the pictures and stories that Crystal had given me to share with our passengers. They loved them. After visiting Ketchikan for the afternoon, we headed out to anchor in a quiet cove for the night.

The next day, we made our way to Wrangell—where, in the harbor, the *Puffin* boat was docked in the very first slip! (I mentioned in the previous chapter, I believed that my late grandfather, Homer, was watching over me, as I had seen the same boat last season in Petersburg. Remember that the license plate on my grandfather's van was *PUFFIN*. Awesome! It was comforting to know that he was still keeping an eye on me as this new cruise season began.)

During the next two months, I had many wonderful experiences traveling on our ship around southeast Alaska. We cruised between various ports, including Juneau, Sitka, Haines, Petersburg, Wrangell, Ketchikan, and Tenakee Springs. On one trip, we saw a massive pod of sixteen Orcas—which in itself is a rare and thrilling sight. (Most pods of Orcas include only three or four family members.) In spite of some rough spots dealing with the crew, this season truly had its exciting moments.

* * *

MAYBE IT WASN'T MEANT TO BE

As our summer journey continued, there was one thing that really bothered me—the lack of time that I had to work on this book. Before we left for Alaska, I'd already written the first eight chapters. My goal was to spend one hour after work each night editing those stories. I also planned to begin writing this chapter in which, originally, I had a different idea. Consequently, I felt that I would have this book ready to publish by the end of the summer.

However, there's one thing that I have definitely learned well in my life. It's that my plans don't always come to fruition in the way that I think they will. Being drained from dealing with continuous turmoil among the crew on our ship and working extra-long hours, I had no energy to spend on this book. So, at the beginning of June, two months had gone by without me writing or editing a single word, and I was feeling discouraged. I began to think that perhaps God had other tasks for me...but soon my spirits would be uplifted.

---

*"Have I not commanded you? Be strong and of good courage;
do not be afraid, nor be dismayed, for the Lord your God is
with you wherever you go."*
[NKJV Bible Joshua 1:9]

Being the cruise host, I was mingling in the ship's intimate lounge with a small group of passengers. One of them was Sue, a woman from Australia. We chatted for a few minutes about her experience on our boat before I asked what she did for a living. She responded that she had been a professional writer for thirty years, and related more about her career accomplishments. After a while, I felt that we had a good connection, so I told Sue about my book and the challenge in getting it completed. I then asked her if perhaps she'd do some editing for me. Sue welcomed the opportunity to help, and over the course of our nine-day cruise, she generously edited the first four chapters—which indeed was a huge help. Apparently, it pays to mingle.

Half of this book had now been reviewed by a seasoned professional writer. Excellent, but what about the next four chapters? On our very next cruise, I would get my answer.

Three of the passengers were sisters, and during a conversation with one of them, Katie, I mentioned my book. She told me that she and her two sisters were all experienced teachers. Katie then said that they would be happy to edit the next four chapters for me. Incredible! I was truly blessed to be getting more professional help with this book.

Over the next few days, Katie and her sisters sat together wherever they could, reading and editing the last four chapters. They, like Sue, did not want any credit or money for their efforts. Although the prior two months had passed without the book moving forward, within a few days, the impasse had clearly broken with the help of *four* professionals. Talk about feeling grateful!

It was now the middle of June, and just as this book was taking shape, our crew was also being reshaped. Three of our more problematic employees were fired. Now one-third of our team was gone. Unfortunately, those changes did not solve all the crew problems. Our second captain, Frank, who guided the ship when Captain Jack was off duty, was not the right guy for the job. He seemed to be lacking in management ability, which came to light more and more each day—a circumstance that led to increased drama and uneasiness within our staff.

A few days into the first cruise with our three new employees, we docked in Petersburg on a Saturday morning. We'd be leaving the following afternoon on Sunday and I was hoping desperately to be able to go to a twelve-step meeting there. Regrettably, I found out that they were only scheduled on Tuesday, Friday, and Sunday nights. So, I was out of luck. My next best option was going to church.

Early Sunday morning, I searched the internet and found one on the outskirts of town. I called a taxi to take me there. After the service, the acting pastor, Ty, came over to me and introduced himself. I asked him if he knew anyone who could give me a ride back to town near our ship. Ty offered to drive me there. (Another wonderful blessing.)

During our short ride, Ty and I began a great conversation. Once in town, he pulled into a parking lot and turned off his truck, which gave us the opportunity to continue talking. Consequently, I told Ty the story (from Chapter 4) about Sadie. He greatly enjoyed me sharing it with him. Fifteen minutes later, our visit ended. I thanked Ty for giving me a ride and stepped out of his truck.

Next, I walked a few feet and went into the grocery store, which had an upstairs area featuring clothing and other household items. I had been in the lower-level food section many times before, but never ventured upstairs. For some reason that day, I decided to go up there.

Immediately upon reaching the top stair, I was stunned. Directly in front of me was a display rack with mini Petersburg street signs featuring various people's names. Staring right at me was the sign, *Sadie Avenue*. Unbelievable! Shocked at what I was seeing, I instantly grabbed the sign and rushed to the counter to buy it. This visit to Petersburg was surely a blessed one.

Leaving the area later that day, we spent the next two weeks cruising to various ports throughout southeast Alaska before arriving in Juneau. It was now the end of June and there was still far too much discord among our crew, which was an unhealthy source of stress for me. Hence, as soon as our boat hit the dock, I rushed up the street to a twelve-step meeting. While talking to some good friends there, they suggested that I needed to quit my job and pursue other employment opportunities in town.

Walking back to our ship, I called Captain Jack, who was down south, and stated that I could no longer work on the ship. I also mentioned that there were three other employees who had their bags packed and were ready to leave. Consequently, if we all quit our jobs, the current cruise would not be able to continue. The ship would be four crew members short of what was needed to be operating properly—according to what Jack had previously told me. The passengers would then lose out on the final three days of their cruise, which was scheduled to end in Petersburg. They would also have to bear the expense of rerouting their flights home out of Juneau. Those experiences would truly be a disappointing note on which to end their Alaskan excursion.

Therefore, after talking to Captain Jack, who promised to make changes when he returned in three days, I decided to continue working for him until we got to Petersburg. I spoke to my fellow disgruntled crew members, and they agreed to stay as well. At the end of the trip, Captain Frank would be off for the next two cruises, allowing Jack time to assess current challenges within our staff.

Unbeknownst to me, God apparently had a bigger purpose for me staying on board. Mere hours after I decided not to leave my job, I had another unique experience. At dinner that night, I went into the dining area to give our passengers a quick two-minute update on the activities scheduled for the next day. As I was finishing, one of our guests started asking me some personal questions. Answering them, I unexpectedly began talking about being one's authentic self. A half an hour later, I was finally finished and received an enthusiastic round of applause from our guests.

The next afternoon, our operations manager, Janet, pulled me aside and said that five guests had told her how much they loved my stories. More importantly, Janet believed that I was her blessing, describing to me how she'd been compromising herself and feeling extremely miserable working on our ship. Janet felt that my unplanned message was meant for her to hear, and said that she, too, wanted to resign from her job. That would have made a total of five of us—had we all left.

Three days later, Captain Jack returned to our ship, and Captain Frank started a two-cruise vacation. In talking to crew members throughout that time, Jack realized that he needed to find another captain to help him finish out our season, as he only skippered about half of our trips throughout the summer. Jack learned that if Frank were to come back to work, at least four employees, including myself, would leave. Surely it was much easier for Jack to replace one captain than several crew members. After all, it was now the middle of the season, and any good crew help would most likely be working somewhere else. Therefore, Frank was replaced with Carl, a very talented captain with plenty of management experience. On the same day, Janet decided not to compromise herself any longer, and moved on to her next adventure.

Unfortunately having Captain Carl on board, even with his years of expertise in supervising various crews, could not eliminate all of the ongoing employee drama. Soon after his arrival, our pastry chef and recently-hired first mate—both of whom were fed up with ongoing grievances—followed suit with Janet and resigned their positions. Overall, between April and September, we had seven new employees replacing the original crew of nine.

Thankfully, skills that I learned in my twelve-step program helped to get me through the trying times. Prayer and meditation were two of those gifts. During my daily moments of reflection, I kept getting strong feelings that God wanted me on our ship for a meaningful purpose—either to accomplish something significant or to learn a valuable lesson.

* * *

BREAKING FROM THE CHAOS

It was now the last week in July and I had been cruising on Captain Jack's boat for nearly four months. I experienced plenty of blessings, but the constant crew chaos still weighed heavily on me.

Our next nine-day trip would start and end in Juneau, a place where I have numerous friends. So I told Jack that I would need to take the next cruise off and stay with one of them. He wasn't excited about that, yet he knew that I was serious about taking care of my serenity; therefore, Jack agreed to the vacation.

My first day off was a Wednesday and I went to three meetings. I also had the opportunity to visit several friends. Thursday held more of the same, along with eating plenty of good Alaskan food. Friday, I had an extremely enjoyable evening.

After attending a meeting, I decided to forgo dinner with friends. Rather, I went to see if I could find a black bear or two at the Mendenhall Glacier. Nearly as soon as I arrived, a large mama bear was fishing in the stream. Jackpot! Her three cubs were just a few feet away on shore. There were about thirty people watching them from the boardwalk. Several minutes later, mama caught a salmon, and led her youngsters onto a small island in the middle of the stream. It appeared that this would be their resting place for the night, as they hid behind some tall grass, out of view of the onlookers. Not surprisingly, the entire crowd decided to leave. I chose to hang out and take in the clean air and invigorating energy around the glacier.

A few minutes later, two wonderful women came and stood near me. We ended up walking the boardwalk together while following another black bear that came strolling by us in the marsh below. That was an awesome way to conclude the evening.

Near the end of my vacation, I met another fantastic woman named Cynthia who became a major blessing to me. Several days before I ran into her, I had broken my camera. Since I'd already been thinking about upgrading it before I broke it, I thought I'd wait to buy a new one until after our season ended. That would give me more time to make a good decision on what model to buy. I shared that story with Cynthia.

By chance, she happened to have the same type of camera that I had been using and offered to let me borrow hers for the next couple of cruises. Our upcoming trips would take us in and out of Juneau a few times so I'd have the opportunity to return it on one of those occasions. Still, I was hesitant to accept Cynthia's generosity because I had only recently met her. Thankfully, I took the camera.

Three days into our next cruise, I was by myself on the rear deck of our boat, facing the Five Finger Lighthouse, which sits on its own small island with some very picturesque scenery. My grandfather, Homer, was noted for a picture that he had taken of a lighthouse on Block Island, Rhode Island. While staring at the landscape in front of me, I had an invigorating thought. Should a humpback whale happen to swim between the lighthouse and me, I would have the opportunity to take an incredible photograph. As my family would say, I'd have a "Homer picture."

Astoundingly, within two minutes of having that thought, a humpback whale came swimming by our ship. It was only about twenty-five yards from me and directly in front of the lighthouse. Excited, I began snapping pictures. After the whale dove down, I quickly checked the images that I had taken with Cynthia's camera. Jackpot! I had captured a perfect snapshot.

I'm an amateur shutterbug and Homer was a multi-award-winning nature photographer. Nevertheless, that day, I was blessed to be in the right place at the right time. Now I have *my* "Homer picture."

Before we left on this adventure, there was another picture-perfect image that caught my eye while I was walking down the dock to board our ship. Parked directly behind us was a large, mega-million-dollar boat named *Serenity.* Seriously?

I had just taken the last cruise off to try and find some serenity, and now it practically hit me in the face. Throughout this trip, we ventured into some fairly secluded areas of southeast Alaska. Somehow, that boat, *Serenity,* ended up next to us in many of those places.

Then something even more intriguing happened when we returned to Juneau. After walking to a twelve-step meeting, I returned to our ship and surprisingly that same boat, *Serenity*, was docked behind us once again. Even more incredible, sitting directly in front of us, was another mega-million-dollar vessel—also named *Serenity*! What are the odds of that happening? One of those ships was registered in the United States, the other in the Virgin Islands. Here I was looking for serenity, and it was literally surrounding me.

The following day, I shared my experience with the two *Serenity* ships at another meeting. One of the ladies there stated something simple, yet profound. She said that it appeared that serenity was with me wherever I went—I simply had to look for it. How right she was.

We were now in the middle of September and, in two days, we'd be leaving Juneau for the last time this season. Our next cruise would be fourteen days to Seattle. Before leaving, I visited Cynthia to return her camera and expressed my appreciation for her friendship and for being such a tremendous blessing.

Along our journey southward, we would visit Petersburg, Wrangell, and Ketchikan before entering Canadian waters. Once there, we'd travel three days non-stop 24/7, as we did not have the necessary permits to stop anywhere in Canada. So we wouldn't dock again until we reached northern Washington and the San Juan Islands.

On a Sunday afternoon, twelve days into our cruise, we made it there and docked for the night in Roche Harbor. This is a quaint little seaport village with plenty of history. President Teddy Roosevelt and John Wayne stayed there at the *Hotel De Haro*. People of wealth bring their incredible yachts to Roche Harbor for the summer season. I'm told by locals that most people need three jobs in order to survive there.

After dinner, our passengers had the opportunity to hop off the ship and visit this quiet, well-landscaped town. Some guests went for a stroll to explore the area; others sat and enjoyed an ice cream cone as the sun set. I decided to go for a walk. As fate would have it,

I ran into two friends from Juneau who were also bringing their boat back to Seattle. We had a great conversation before I headed back to my cabin to get some rest.

The next morning, Monday, I guided some of our more energetic guests on an exhilarating hike. Along the way, we saw several of the area's most prominent natural residents—black-tailed deer. After returning from the approximately one-hour walk, I took a quick shower.

Then it was time for the passengers to enjoy a scheduled bus tour around San Juan Island—all except for an eighty-one-year-old man named David, who said he wasn't feeling well.

I traveled along on this excursion, and we stopped at several places of interest, including an alpaca farm, an orca viewing area, and a lavender estate. The bus driver added to our experience by sharing some interesting island history.

As we were on the tour, Captain Jack was driving our ship to the other side of San Juan Island to an area known as Friday Harbor. Compared to Roche Harbor, it's a bustling town, though still an intimate and very popular tourist destination. There are numerous shops, restaurants, and activities available. The ferry there shuttles passengers to other San Juan Islands and mainland Washington.

Nearly three hours after it began, our tour around the island came to an end in Friday Harbor. There, we would eventually board our ship, which was still making its way to the docking area. Meanwhile, the guests had the opportunity to visit the town for about an hour. I sat on a bench in front of the dock to relax and take in the fresh air and blue skies.

Finally, our vessel had arrived and it was time to hop onboard, eat lunch, and head to Seattle. We'd be there approximately six hours after we began cruising, bringing an end to our fourteen-day journey from Juneau.

* * *

A BLESSED FINAL JOURNEY

As the sun glistened gorgeously off of the harbor water, Captain Jack sounded our ship's horn. Seattle, here we come. The day couldn't have been more magnificent. A clear, brilliant blue sky hung above us; the air was fresh and clean, and a crisp, fall breeze blew around us. This was the perfect way to end our cruise.

Oh, but not so fast.

The answer to the BIG question why God wanted me to stay on the ship this summer was finally about to be revealed.

We left Friday Harbor on Monday afternoon around two-thirty and began our relatively short voyage to Seattle. Most of the passengers were relaxing on the boat's outside decks, enjoying the beauty of the day. One passenger, though, did not join the rest of them. David, the same guest who decided not to take part in the morning bus tour, was resting in his room.

About forty-five minutes into our journey, this perfect day took an ominous turn. I was in the upstairs dining area working on the computer. Suddenly, looking stressed and acting with urgency, a female crew member asked me to bring a bag of ice to David's room. She had just exited the ship's bridge only a few feet from me, and most likely had told Captain Jack of David's situation. I had no idea what was happening with him, but obviously it didn't seem good.

Quickly finding a plastic bag, I filled it with ice and raced downstairs to David's room. He was sitting upright on his bed with his back against the wall. Judy, his wife, was standing at the foot of the bed. One of the passengers was a retired pastor, and Judy asked me to bring her down to see David. Two nurses were also cruising with us. Both of them had already begun checking David's vital signs. I gave one of the nurses the bag of ice and rushed to find the pastor.

When she and I made it back to David, a nurse was giving him a cup of ginger ale, from which he took a sip. Immediately afterward, I saw his eyes roll back into his head, and he became motionless. (I thought to myself, *this can't be good*; *did I just watch David die?*) At this point, I felt that I couldn't be of any more assistance there and didn't want to get in the way, so I left the room to allow the professionals to tend to him.

I ran upstairs to the bridge to give Captain Jack an update on what was happening. He was on our emergency phone talking with the Coast Guard. They were sending a rescue boat to meet us, as we had already turned back towards Friday Harbor. Feeling the adrenaline running intensely through my veins, our sense of urgency was sky-high, as I stood near Jack awaiting the Coast Guard.

Their small skiff traveled about ten miles per hour faster than our ship. Therefore, it was decided that when they met up with us, they would transfer David to their vessel in order to get him more medical help sooner. That plan changed, however, about fifteen minutes later when the Coast Guard crew reached our boat. After their initial examination of David, they immediately began CPR on him, and told us to continue driving the ship at full throttle until we reached Friday Harbor. As we charged ahead, the two members of the Coast Guard valiantly continued their efforts to revive David.

Arriving at Friday Harbor at about four o'clock, a team of twelve medical professionals was awaiting us on the dock. Members of the Port Authority were also there to help us tie up our boat. David's unconscious body was now on a stretcher in the hallway at mid-ship. Once our vessel was secured, the medics hopped on board and instantly went to work. They diligently performed CPR on David, administered fluids through an IV, and applied defibrillating shocks.

I stood only four feet away from the team and I was thoroughly impressed with their relentless professionalism. Such controlled chaos! Their efforts were like a well-oiled machine and, yes, it's their job, I know—but I could not help but feel they were passionately rooting for David. They seemed to be going above and beyond, doing everything they possibly could to bring him back.

After about twenty minutes of intently working to save David, the head nurse announced that they would try one more round of CPR. If they did not get a pulse, she was going to call off their efforts. Regrettably, after that final attempt to resuscitate David, she uttered the heartbreaking words, "That's it, I'm ceasing this operation. The time is now 4:29 p.m. Thank you, everyone."

Sadly, David had passed away—but that's not the end of this story.

With his lifeless body lying on a stretcher, it was time for the preliminary investigation. Judy, now a widow, had to answer questions from various authorities. A sheriff came on board, along with a county prosecutor, the coroner, and an investigator for the Coast Guard. Judy was asked the same questions by all four of them. They needed to make sure that she had not done something to cause David's death. In today's world, it's necessary for everyone to cover their bases. After about an hour, at five thirty p.m., the inquiry ended and Judy was ready for a few moments alone.

I asked the coroner and the county prosecutor what would happen next. Remember, we were on a small island. They told me that they'd be putting David on the next ferry out of town, which was leaving in less than an hour at six thirty. I asked why they wouldn't be handling him at Friday Harbor. The coroner replied that once someone dies, they take the body immediately to the nearest funeral home—which, in this case, was an *hour-long* ferry ride away to Anacortes. Yes, that's the same Anacortes where I hung out with my new friend Otis back in April.

Captain Jack asked me to accompany Judy and her friends, Phil and Mary, on the ferry as they rode along with David's body. I immediately called Otis and told him of our situation. He recommended a hotel for us, and offered to pick us up at the ferry terminal in Anacortes. Incredible!

I gave Jack the hotel information so that he could make arrangements for the four of us. Then Judy, Phil, Mary, and I each grabbed an overnight bag and took a short walk to the ferry. David's body was already on board in a minivan, not a hearse, so as not to alarm any passengers that a deceased person was traveling with them.

The four of us boarded the ferry and decided to walk up to the top deck. Judy found a seat outside with Phil and Mary sitting on one side of her, while I sat on the other. A solid steel wall about four feet high, which prevented passengers from falling off the ship, was directly in front of us. Therefore, we couldn't see our boat from our seats even though it was docked only fifty yards away. As we waited to depart, I received a text from one of our passengers. She said that everyone was waiting on the back deck to wave good-bye to Judy. I replied that I would bring her to the ferry's rail as soon as we started our journey.

A few minutes later, we began the short trip to Anacortes. Judy and I walked to the railing while everyone on our cruise ship was waving to her. I heard several shouts of "We love you, Judy!" As the ferry continued on its route, Judy and I remained standing against the railing, shoulder to shoulder. That's when the meaning of our excursion really came alive for me.

Judy started to tell me that although she was terribly sad, she also felt a sense of comfort with David's passing. She related that he had never wanted anything to do with God throughout his life. Judy continued saying that only one month prior to David's passing, she suggested that he start praying—and that his response was anything but positive. David told Judy that he would be a hypocrite if he prayed; however, she responded with something profound:

"If you pray and there's no God, you lose nothing because you don't believe in Him anyway; but if there *is* a God, you gain the whole world."

David had no immediate response, yet Judy quietly prayed that her husband might soon change his mind.

"...and whatever you ask in prayer,
you will receive, if you have faith."
[ESV Bible Matthew 21:22]

Still sharing her story with me, Judy claimed that two weeks after she suggested prayer to David, he actually came to her saying that he had, indeed, been praying for the last two weeks. Judy was completely stunned yet extremely grateful. After more than sixty years of marriage, her longtime prayer had been answered. David also indicated that he was praying for only *one* thing: that whenever his time came to leave this world, he wanted to go quickly. Sadly, just two weeks after sharing that news with Judy, he passed away—his only prayer now answered. Although mournful, Judy felt immense peace with this knowledge. She believed that David was now being well taken care of by his loving Father in Heaven.

Judy then shared some interesting facts. David had a challenging personality. Even though he was a very successful businessman with many associates, he had only one friend. It was Phil, who happened to be on board with us, along with his wonderful wife, Mary. David had talked them into coming on this cruise only about a week before it began. So, amazingly, when he passed away, David had his loving wife and his only friend with him. There were also two nurses and a recently retired pastor as guests on our ship. Even more, David had just spent nine of the last thirteen days of his life in Alaska, aka, "God's Country." Most importantly, his only prayer (to die quickly) was answered. Hopefully, we'll all be that blessed when each of us comes to our last day.

Continuing on, Judy told me that David's and her favorite things to do were to watch sunsets and moons. When we began our ferry ride from Friday Harbor, the sky was a light pink color and shortly afterward it turned intense orange. That brought peace to all four of us—Judy, Phil, Mary, and me—as there was no doubt in our minds that David was showing us a glimpse of Heaven. While his body was three decks below us, his spirit shined brightly above.

We also noticed that over a mountain directly in front of us had risen a full, radiantly orange moon. Looking at that magnificent orb, Judy was now certain that David was letting her know that he was at peace.

About seventy-five minutes after it began, our ride across the waters of the San Juan Islands had come to an end at the ferry terminal in Anacortes. The four of us waited on board, watching as they unloaded all the vehicles below. We were hoping to see the minivan carrying David's body as it exited the ferry. However, since it had no markings, we couldn't tell which one it was. Disappointed, about twenty minutes after our journey ended, we headed off the ferry.

As I expected, Otis was right there in the terminal waiting for us. Some short introductions and hugs took place, and then we all walked to Otis's truck. It was the same one that he let me borrow back in April. Once we were all in the vehicle, a beautiful doe appeared and stood staring at us from only a few feet away. We sat and watched it, which brought Judy even more peace. Moments later, the deer turned and walked into the woods. Otis started his truck and we headed to our hotel.

The ride there took about twenty minutes, and it was now just after nine. We were staying in downtown Anacortes at the Majestic Inn & Spa. *Absolutely extraordinary* is how I would describe the staff there. Their caring customer service could not have been any better. The ladies at the front desk, Amity and PK, had reserved an incredible suite for Judy. They even gave her a wonderful card honoring David. Amity's and PK's compassion and thoughtfulness were just what Judy needed after such a trying day.

Otis had also endured a challenging afternoon, so he declined my invitation to join us for dinner and headed home. What a blessing he had been to us all.

After paying a short visit to our rooms, Judy, Phil, Mary, and I met in the hotel restaurant for dinner, as we were starving. Although they were closing the kitchen, the staff were nice enough to make sure that we could get a delicious meal. I was so grateful to be eating with my new friends. Feeling Judy's joy as she shared stories of herself and David was wonderful, yet sad. I felt tremendously blessed that I had been chosen to assist her during this trying time.

Early the next morning at six thirty, I went for a walk on Commercial Avenue, the main street that goes through the center of Anacortes. Looking to my right, I saw a white full moon in the sky and also noticed a building which had a barren flag pole on its roof with a horizontal piece of metal across its midsection. From my perspective, it looked like a large cross sitting in front of the moon. I immediately felt a warm sense that David was thanking me for taking care of Judy and that he wanted me to tell her he was doing great. It was truly a powerful experience.

Wanting to remember this moment, I grabbed my cellphone and snapped a photo of this extraordinary scene.

As I continued my walk, I made another intriguing discovery. Just a few feet further on Commercial Avenue, there was only one car parked—an older-model, off-white sedan. *JESUS 4 [YOU]* was decaled in dark blue on both the hood and the sides of the car. (The YOU was represented by a closed fist with the index finger pointing straight ahead.) I quickly snapped a picture of the car and tears began to fill my eyes. At that moment, I was feeling extremely emotional as I looked in the sky and asked God why He chose me to be His agent to help Judy.

Returning to the hotel, I met Judy, Phil, and Mary for breakfast in the restaurant. Sitting down, I excitedly shared what I had experienced on my walk and then showed them the pictures that I took. Each of us now had a definite belief that God was truly taking care of David.

As could be expected, Judy was anxious to get to the funeral parlor and see David one last time. She also needed to make arrangements for his cremation before flying home to the Midwest. However, Judy couldn't do either until the coroner examined David's body. Normal procedure in these cases requires the accurate determination of "cause of death" to rule out anything unusual. While no one expected any surprises, we would have to wait a bit longer for the matter to be resolved completely. We all prayed that it would not be a lengthy process.

At approximately eight that morning, Judy called Joe, the funeral director, who said that he had not yet heard from the coroner's office. Fortunately, it was only a bit more than an hour later when Joe phoned Judy with the update. He said that the coroner determined that David's passing was consistent with his advanced age and the medications that he was taking. Accordingly, his death was ruled to be the result of coronary disease. Judy, as were we all, was so relieved that this news came early. Now we could make our visit to the funeral home.

In order to get there, we all hopped into a taxi and rode about three miles up Commercial Avenue. Upon arrival, we were greeted by Joe, who led us into a small conference room and offered us something to drink. Joe and Judy then went over the paperwork for David's cremation while Phil, Mary, and I sat at the table with them. When they were done, Judy asked Joe to let her see David one last time. He rejected her request, stating that David's body wasn't in any condition for her to view. Joe did not want Judy to have a sad last memory of her husband.

With plenty of frustration in her voice, Judy demanded that Joe allow her to see David. Politely yet firmly, Joe repeated his answer, "No." He said that there were numerous marks on David's face, he still had intravenous catheters in him, his body was covered with a sheet, and it wasn't something that Joe wanted Judy to see. It was also policy that family members not be permitted to see the decedent until they are duly prepared for viewing.

Despite Joe's objection, there was no way that I was going to let Judy take no for an answer. I felt the need to make sure that she received what she wanted, but did not want to cause a confrontation. Sitting right next to Joe, I turned and looked him straight in the eyes and asked him with an intent *albeit* diplomatic tone, "Comfortably for you, how long would it take to get just David's face ready? You can leave his body covered. She just needs to see his face."

The look in Joe's eyes told me he realized that we were not about to leave until he appeased Judy's request. It was now only ten thirty. A few seconds later Joe responded, saying, "Come back in an hour and a half, and I'll have him ready." Hearing that, Judy expressed an enormous sigh of relief. The rest of us did as well.

We then called a taxi to take us back to our hotel in order to check out. On arrival, Judy's son, Ben, called from Tennessee, saying that he secured a rental car for me to drive the four of us back to our ship. It was now docked in Ballard, about two hours south of us. The rental car, however, would not be available for a couple of hours. Accordingly, just before noon, we took a taxi back to the funeral parlor so that Judy could say goodbye to her partner of more than sixty years.

Joe greeted us and then escorted Judy into the private viewing area where her husband's body was resting. After about ten minutes, she emerged from the room. I imagined that Judy would be quite somber after seeing David for the last time—but surprisingly, she appeared rather exuberant. Judy then expressed her relief and joy that Joe had done such masterful work with David. She said that his face looked amazing—that he looked better than she could ever have expected.

Phil and Mary went in next. They came out and reiterated Judy's sentiment. I declined to visit David because I really didn't know him. Having helped Judy get to see her husband one last time was good enough for me. Witnessing the joy in the eyes of my three friends, I thanked Joe for his great skill, and acknowledged his dedication and commitment to Judy.

With our mission accomplished, the four of us each thanked Joe for his efforts. He then gave us a ride to a local sandwich shop as we all needed some extra energy before our two-hour drive back to the ship. While we were eating, a representative from the rental car agency arrived with our vehicle. Once finished with our lunch, it was time to say goodbye to Anacortes.

But not quite yet....

I stated earlier in this chapter that back in April when I had Otis's truck, I was able to discover Cap Santé Park. It's a small viewing area that overlooks Fidalgo Island (home to the city of Anacortes) and some of the other San Juan islands. After lunch, I told Judy that I had someplace special to show her before we left town. She agreed to ride with me, along with Phil and Mary, so the four of us hopped in our rental car. Giving them no indication of where we were going, I drove us up the winding road towards Cap Santé Park.

Once there, I exited our car and asked Judy to follow me. I led her over to a panoramic spot near the rocky cliff overlooking all of

Anacortes, its surrounding waters, and the landscape below. My hope was to give Judy a gift by showing her something truly magnificent.

As Judy and I looked straight ahead, I pointed to the mountain on the island across the channel—above which we had seen the spectacular orange moon the night before. With my arm around her shoulders, I turned her to the left, and showed her the terminal below, where the minivan carrying David's body had exited the ferry. Judy remained quiet and subdued, while tears began to fill *my* eyes.

I paused to accentuate the moment, took a deep breath, and invited Judy to look down at the gorgeous blue waters below. The view before her entailed the actual route of the ferry on which she had traveled the night before. That's right, the very last journey that she and David—her lifelong companion and soulmate—had taken together. I then walked a short distance away, leaving her alone to embrace the view and experience the moment.

Having watched how small and painful her life quickly became yesterday afternoon, it was my hope to help console Judy by providing a larger perspective, or the "big picture," of the environment in which last night's events occurred. Given the unexpected and untimely death of her partner, I believed that this experience would bring her some peace and closure.

Several minutes later, Judy returned to the car, composed, satisfied, and at peace. She thanked me lovingly for bringing her to the park—which I had discovered only because of Otis's generosity back in April. At that moment I realized what a missed opportunity this would have been had he and I not connected six months earlier.

With all of our personal business done, it was time to drive to our ship in north Seattle. Nearly three hours later, at about five thirty in the evening, we arrived there. We would have made it sooner, but I missed a few turns.

Judy insisted that I join her for dinner. Showing a greater sense of ease and humor, she jokingly stated that I could order whatever I wanted because she would be paying the bill with David's money. Sharing a quick laugh with Judy, I accepted her offer, as I certainly was not going to pass up my last opportunity to spend time with this incredible woman of faith. Phil and Mary decided to join us and we all walked up the dock to a prominent seafood restaurant.

During our meal, Judy thanked me for helping her with David's arrangements. She then looked me in the eyes and said, "God could not have sent a better man to help me." Phil and Mary quickly echoed Judy's sentiment. Wow. My eyes welled up as their comments left me speechless.

Once finished with our delicious meal and wonderful fellowship, the four of us headed back to our ship for a night of rest. In the morning, I had a car service drive Judy to the airport in Seattle. Phil and Mary were picked up by a family member. Finally, it was the end of a remarkable journey.

At last, I had the BIG answer as to why God wanted me to stay on our ship all summer—which was to be of service to Judy during what was arguably the saddest and most difficult time of her life.

* * *

As I now reflect upon the story of that summer's journey, I find it truly incredible. It was a six-month adventure of awe-inspiring moments and improbable "coincidences." Surely it was a story that I could never have predicted or even imagined—yet an adventure so masterfully designed and perfectly delivered that I had to share it with you.

Coincidence?

I say NOT!

EPILOGUE: BEYOND A REASONABLE DOUBT

My hope is that the stories in this book have touched your hearts in some positive way. I say this having experienced firsthand the reaction of dozens of people with whom I have shared them. Most prominently, I received numerous wonderfully unexpected responses when I related the events that I wrote about in Chapter 9 to a group of spiritually minded people. Many of them expressed to me that the story needs to become a faith-based film.

On a Monday afternoon, a few days before I penned these final thoughts for this book, I was praying to God because I had been asked to speak at a twelve-step meeting that coming Wednesday. The get-together is attended by many who have long-term sobriety— that is, thirty, forty, fifty-plus years or so. Although I'm currently twenty-seven years sober, I was wondering what I could impart that would resonate with the attendees' hearts. They obviously did not need me telling them how our recovery program worked.

All of a sudden, I was hit with a strong notion that I needed to talk to that group about God. Immediately questioning that thought, I dropped to my knees and asked Him for clarification. The second that

I asked God for help, a notification sounded on my cellphone, indicating I'd received a text message. It was from my friend Jane, who had booked me to speak at that upcoming meeting. Her text read:

"Reminder: You are speaking Weds at Colfax Ave Try God."

Seriously! I received this message specifically telling me to TRY GOD at the exact same time that I was praying to Him for an answer. This response could not have been any more straightforward, direct, or immediate. It so reminds me of the time I mentioned in Chapter 6, when my friend, Pastor Larry, sent me a text with the answer I was seeking from God—just as I was praying at *that* moment.

Here's the interesting part of that scenario with Jane. I knew that she was a very spiritual woman. Therefore, I believed that her text was giving me a hint of what to share about—God. However, when I arrived to speak on Wednesday, Jane handed me a three-ring binder and asked me to look over the meeting's format. At the top of the first page, in large bold letters, it said **TRY GOD**. I looked at Jane and said, "That's weird." She asked me what I meant. I told her about the "coincidence" of the message that she had sent me saying TRY GOD.

Jane then explained to me that TRY GOD was the name of that meeting. I had a quick laugh. For years, I had always thought that its name was the "Universal" because it used to be held on the back lot at Universal Studios. I never knew that it was named TRY GOD. Without knowing, I had already prepared what I was going to discuss with the group—the story of Otis, Judy, and David.

I had only ten minutes to share that summer-long adventure of how a coincidental meeting with a new acquaintance positioned me to be able to support and comfort another new friend after the tragic loss of her husband.

My audience was nearly one hundred strong as I narrated that story, describing all that transpired during that summer. Watching them during my delivery, everyone was leaning forward with their chins in their hands, sitting enrapt, looking intently at me, awaiting each next thing that I shared.

At the end of my story, I noticed something profound. Nearly all of the people in the room had tears in their eyes. In such a group with so many years of sobriety—a group that has "heard it all before"—you rarely encounter an instance where a tale like this evokes such a heartfelt response. After the meeting, numerous attendees came up to thank me for the blessing they received from what they heard.

Then, unexpectedly, just before I left the room, a woman walked up to me, shook my hand, and said, "I was the one that you came here to share that story with today." Thanking me, she turned and quickly made her way to the door. My eyes instantaneously became moist. I wasn't exactly sure how I felt—although that was more proof to me that I was supposed to write this book. Clearly, my mistaken understanding of Jane's text about TRY GOD was not a coincidence.

If you're a believer, I have to imagine that your mind is racing right now. It's probably going at warped speed as you recall your own fascinating God-filled instances. Events so convincing and miraculous that you had to witness them to believe them, ones that have left you with absolutely no doubt that God exists.

Perhaps you were a non-believer before you read this book. After reading the stories in it, I cannot imagine that you haven't come to believe in God. At least a little. However, if you still have not, please allow me to recap the evidence that I have presented.

I'll start with the story in Chapter 9, since it's probably the freshest one in your mind. Evidently, it took David nearly eighty-two years to change his thoughts about praying to God. Blessedly, it happened one month before he passed away, when he had his only prayer answered—to go quickly and peacefully when his time came. Seemingly, God waited patiently all those years for David to come to Him and, when he finally did, God was right there waiting for him.

As I have shown throughout this book, God certainly does listen to prayers, and He would most assuredly listen to yours as well. If you doubt otherwise (like David did), why not try? What have you got to lose?

If there truly were no God in this world, how would you explain the story of Anthony (Chapter 2), the young man that my ex-wife and I were planning to adopt? There were so many intricate parts involved in creating that almost unbelievable episode. It was so meticulously set up, even Hollywood could not have produced a better script.

There were also the almost unimaginable occurrences that I experienced in Chapter 3. Incredibly, I came upon those two I LOVE YOU messages written in the sand thousands of miles apart. Remember, I saw each of them the day after I prayed to God about what direction I should take in my life.

Then there's Chapter 4 with the story of the coins, Sadie's song, and The Spinners. The construction of that tale was an absolute masterpiece. It continues to mesmerize me how precise every little detail of that adventure was—from the time I left Alaska to watching The Spinners on stage in Palm Springs.

I'm getting drained just thinking about the unbelievable number of "coincidences" in this book. So, rather than recapping the other chapters, it's time for my final piece of testimony. The one that I pray will help you to believe in God, at least a little.

You may remember something important from reading Chapter 1. I never grew up dreaming of promoting God in any way. Yes, I was introduced to Him by my late great-grandmother, Mabel. Then, for a couple of years, I served as an acolyte in my hometown church. Nevertheless, once my life got busy, I almost immediately ignored

God. I believed He no longer was an asset to me, rather He was a liability. Taking care of my school responsibilities, playing baseball, and participating in other activities became my priorities.

Throughout the next three and a half decades, I had an up-and-down relationship with God—never truly seeking an intimate relationship with Him. Then, my now ex-wife convinced me to go back to church. That's when I started re-examining my thoughts about God. For reasons that I cannot explain, I began to believe in Him on a stronger level. Even so, I still hadn't developed an incredible closeness with God.

I did, though, begin to oversee the homeless ministry at a megachurch in Orange County. Then I began producing and hosting a popular worldwide internet radio program, *In Your Face*. I also wrote my first God-themed book: *God, Bless America...Before It's Too Late*. My life's testimony was seen on two major Christian TV shows, *The 700 Club* and *Hour of Power*. Additionally, my wife, kids, and I attended church on a regular basis. It definitely seemed like I was *all-in* for God. However, in hindsight, I was unaware that something was missing that kept me from having a truly intimate relationship with Him. What that was, I'm not sure.

Yet, once my marriage was ending, I began seeing numerous "God signs" on a steady basis, which have continued throughout the past several years. As a result, it has become overwhelmingly clear to me that God is intimately watching over my life, and that I had to write this book. Finally, it was time for me to glorify Him and to share with you how intense and miraculous are the messages that He regularly sends me.

What I have now learned is this: no matter how hard and often I tried to keep God out of my life, He never left me. Not once did God ever turn His back on me, even when I was at the lowest point in my life—when I had poisoned my body with so much alcohol and illegal drugs that I wanted to die.

IS IT GOD OR COINCIDENCE?

Time after time, God has shown me that He is truly faithful and amazingly patient with me. When I genuinely desired to have Him in my life, God began to powerfully show me how glorious He was in so many astounding ways—just as He did for David—who finally sought Him after nearly eighty-two years.

My experience has revealed to me that God is available to us all day, every day, if we seek Him. Whether we have sworn off God or simply refused to acknowledge Him seems to be of no concern to God. How marvelous that we do not have to *do* anything incredible to have Him in our lives. As I've detailed in this book, I believe all we have to do is *open our eyes to see Him.* Many of us, however, are so focused on ourselves and our busy lives that we miss out on the wonder of God.

These stories are only a select few from the numerous unprecedented events that He manifests to help me to constantly realize His presence in my life. God's ways are always so unexpected, making it impossible for me to even imagine what He will orchestrate next. Only God knows the answer. My job is simply to enjoy the ride—recognizing that these events are crafted by the Master's hand, and perfectly delivered.

In the end, I would simply ask two questions:

1) Were all of the stories in this book merely one incredible coincidence after another?

(*I say NOT!*)

2) Is it just coincidence that you are reading this book?

(*Again, I say it's NOT!*)

In fact, I would say... *It's God, Not Coincidence!*

Rob Ekno

END